INVASION presents a wealth of original photographs and provocative insights in its review of the background and principal events of the December 20, 1989, to January 3, 1990, U.S. military operation in Panama.

Military professionals, political specialists, and Panama buffs each get something of lasting value in this single volume that describes the invasion of Panama from three different perspectives:

- **As an important event in the unfolding history of Panama**—through nearly 100 color and more than 60 black and white photographs.

- **As a climactic moment in recent U.S./Panamanian relations**—in narratives that tell how the Bush Administration protected American lives, enforced the Panama Canal treaties, restored democracy to the country, and brought General Noriega to justice.

- **As a fresh chapter in America's military experience**—through the observations and research of an experienced Pentagon correspondent who places the Panama invasion into context.

This book results from the combined efforts of David S. Behar, a Panamanian businessman who shot more than 6,000 photographs during the U.S. military invasion of Panama; Godfrey Harris, an American foreign policy consultant with extensive experience in Panamanian affairs; and Ross W. Simpson, a network radio correspondent who covered Operation Just Cause.

DAVID S. BEHAR has been involved in real estate, finance, and wholesale services in Panama for the past 25 years and was able to utilize his intimate knowledge of the people and the country to get most of the memorable photographs seen in INVASION.

GODFREY HARRIS is a former university instructor, U.S. diplomat, and member of the President's Executive Office. He has written extensively on Panama, including Panama's Position and The Panamanian Perspective, and has long provided political advice to various U.S. and Panamanian organizations.

ROSS W. SIMPSON reports on national affairs for the NBC radio network and the Mutual Broadcasting System from his base in Washington, DC. Besides Panama, Simpson recently covered Nelson Mandela in South Africa, Hurricane Hugo in North Carolina, and the wildfires in Yellowstone National Park.

INVASION

U.S. ARMY RANGERS, based at Hunter Army Airfield in Georgia, wait in cold weather to board a C-141 aircraft for the December 19, 1989 flight to and air drop over Panama.

INVASION

THE AMERICAN DESTRUCTION OF THE NORIEGA REGIME IN PANAMA

Principal Photography by David S. Behar
Narrative Written by Godfrey Harris

Prologue and Epilogue by Ross W. Simpson

THE AMERICAS GROUP
9200 Sunset Blvd., Suite 404
Los Angeles, California 90069
U.S.A.

ISBN:
0-935047-10-7

Library of Congress Catalog Card Number:

90-080776

LIBRARY OF CONGRESS
Library of Congress Cataloging-In-Publication Data

Invasion: the American destruction of the Noriega regime in Panama/
    principal photography by David S. Behar: narrative written by Godfrey
    Harris: prologue and epilogue by Ross W. Simpson. — 1st ed.
        p144. cm.
    Includes bibliographical references.
    ISBN 0-9S5047-10-7:
    1. Panama—History—American invasion, 1989. 2. Panama—History-Ameri
    can Invasion, 1989—Pictorial wcrks. 3. United States-
    -Military policy. I. Behar, David S., 1938- II. Harris,
    Godfrey, 1937- .
    F1567.I58 1990
    972.8705'3—dc20
                                                                90-392
                                                                CIP

PRINTED IN THE UNITED STATES OF AMERICA
by
Penguin Printing

Project Coordinator and Editor
GODFREY HARRIS
Design and Graphics Consultant
JOHN POWERS

In Memory

of the

Soldiers

and

Citizens

Who Lost

Their Lives

During the

1989

American Invasion

of

Panama

ALSO BY GODFREY HARRIS

The Ultimate Black Book

The Panamanian Perspective

Promoting International Tourism (with Kenneth M. Katz)

Commercial Translations (with Charles Sonabend)

From Trash to Treasure (with Barbara DeKovner-Mayer)

Panama's Position

The Quest for Foreign Affairs Officers (with Francis Fielder)

The History of Sandy Hook, New Jersey

Outline of Social Sciences

Outline of Western Civilization

ALSO BY ROSS W. SIMPSON

The Fires of 88

Maryland: A Photographic Celebration

TABLE OF CONTENTS

THIS BOOK REVIEWS THE INVASION OF PANAMA FROM THREE DIFFERENT PERSPECTIVES:

As an important event in the unfolding history of Panama— through the photographs;

As a climactic moment in recent U.S./Panamanian relations—in the narrative; and

As a fresh chapter in America's military experience—in the Prologue and Epilogue.

PANAMA CITY'S SKYLINE *as it looked on the evening before the American invasion. Just beyond the tall Banco Exterior building on Avenida Balboa—easily identifiable in the center of the photograph by the sail motif sculpted on its side—is the American Embassy. The picture looks west toward the Panama Canal.*

PROLOGUE: *"LET'S DO IT!"*

"He's gone too far," President George Bush concluded as he ordered the use of military force to destroy the Panamanian regime of General Manuel Antonio Noriega. "Enough is enough."

RANGERS CHECKING GEAR AND CAMOUFLAGE PAINT *as their aircraft approaches the jump zone over Panama.*

Operation Just Cause, the largest use of U.S. forces in more than 15 years, was in motion. Fifty-three hours after that Sunday meeting in the White House, more than 9,500 soldiers, sailors, marines, and air force personnel joined 13,000 Americans already stationed in Panama for the invasion.

Not since World War II had an airborne operation of this magnitude been attempted. In the early morning hours of December 20, 1989, as many as 285 fixed-wing aircraft and 110 helicopters were maneuvering in the skies over Panama.

THE DIFFICULTY OF URBAN AREA COMBAT *confronts this U.S. soldier as he picks his way among the houses of a residential neighborhood in Panama City.*

Declared Pfc. Louis O. Miller III: "All you were thinking about was saving yourself and your buddies and taking those motherfuckers out, and that's what we did." All told, it took less than six hours to decapitate the Panamanian dictatorship.

Air Force AC-130H gunships—the awesome SPECTRE that Panamanian soldiers called the "Devil in Disguise" and American troops nicknamed the "American Express Card" (Don't leave home without it)—"prepped" the Comandancia complex for ten minutes prior to the initial assault. The complex was the military headquarters of the Panamanian Defense Forces (PDF). Despite the overwhelming pounding from the air and ground, defenders at the compound were not silenced.

POWERFUL TELEVISION CAMERAS *used to aim SPECTRE's guns.*

SPENT SHELL CASINGS *from 20mm cannon litter a bin inside SPECTRE.*

THE SPECTRE *is an Air Force flying gun platform. Seen protruding from the right side of the plane is the red snout of a 105mm howitzer and the barrel of a 40mm Bofors gun. Between the two weapons is a bubble housing electronic gear. The plane moves slowly, but operates with devastating effect.*

"As my APCs (Armored Personnel Carriers) began rolling into the area, the PDF leaned over the balconies of two high rise buildings and began firing AKs (AK-47 assault rifles) straight down at us," said Col. Mike Snell, commander of the 193rd Infantry Brigade. Second Lieutenant Douglas Rubin, commander of the lead assault platoon, added: "Two of my tracks were hit by RPGs (rocket propelled grenades) and put out of action as we ran a gauntlet of fire in front of the Comandancia."

While a Sheridan tank blasted the Comandancia at point-blank range with 152mm cannon rounds, the wall surrounding the headquarters was finally breached with two

THE EL CHORRILLO AREA surrounding the Comandancia shown after the shelling and subsequent fires had subsided.

thundering blasts more than three hours after the attack was launched. By then, disabled and abandoned armored vehicles littered the street in front of the complex. Private First Class Miller was awarded the Bronze Star for zig-zagging through a hail-storm of 40mm grenades and machine gun bullets to get to one APC. He was able to back it off and put its .50 calibre machine gun back into action. Said his First Sergeant later: "The kid's a regular Audie Murphy."

After the fierce fight at the Comandancia, much of the opposition melted away or was isolated by U.S. tactics. More than 5,000 suspected members of the PDF were captured and detained during the invasion—the largest such operation since the Korean War.

MANY PDF SOLDIERS *changed to civilian clothes to try to evade capture.*

THE COMANDANCIA—*headquarters of the Panamanian Defense Forces—was one of the principal points of the American attack.*

PAITILLA AIRPORT, *near the center of Panama City, is illuminated by a flare in the early hours of the invasion.*

GENERAL NORIEGA'S PRIVATE LEAR JET *was kept in a luxuriously appointed hangar at Paitilla Airport where it was attacked.*

General Noriega's Lear jet was another principal target during the first hours of the invasion. A twenty-man Navy SEAL (sea, air and land) team was given the mission of blocking an escape by air. Sources close to the SEALS said that they "got caught" in the open on a ramp at Punta Paitilla Airport and were gunned down by PDF soldiers on duty in and around the plane's special hangar.

"We could have nailed the hell out of them, but we never got a call," said Colonel George A. Gray, commander of the unit deploying the SPECTREs. "All the crew of the gun ship orbiting Punta Paitilla could do was watch helplessly on its low-light-level TV cameras as the SEALS got hosed." It is thought that secure FM radios may have been damaged during the waterborne assault on the airport; by the time the radio operator had switched to a backup UHF system, thirteen members of the unit had died or been wounded.

NORIEGA'S WELL-TRAVELED PLANE (the flags of nations visited are visible on the side of the fuselage) was grounded in the fierce fighting. Note how the windows popped out from the force of the explosions and the bullet holes visible through the back of the hangar.

INVASION

Despite the high cost of Operation Just Cause, it succeeded in removing General Manuel A. Noriega from power.

Ross W. Simpson

23 AMERICANS DIED *in the invasion. One is honored in Panama before his final flight home to the United States.*

INTRODUCTION

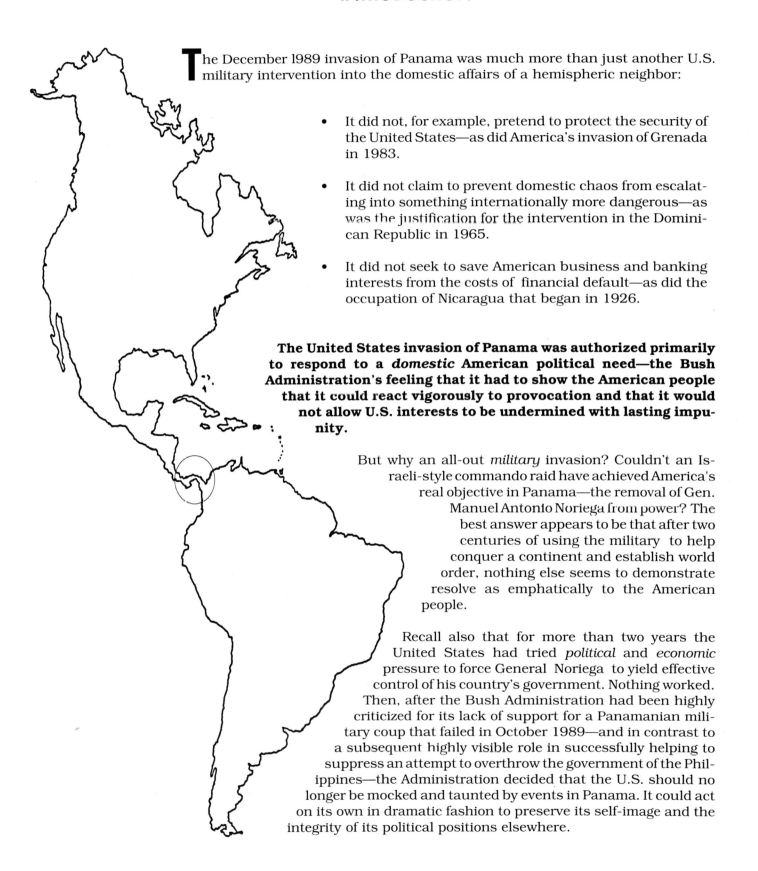

The December 1989 invasion of Panama was much more than just another U.S. military intervention into the domestic affairs of a hemispheric neighbor:

- It did not, for example, pretend to protect the security of the United States—as did America's invasion of Grenada in 1983.

- It did not claim to prevent domestic chaos from escalating into something internationally more dangerous—as was the justification for the intervention in the Dominican Republic in 1965.

- It did not seek to save American business and banking interests from the costs of financial default—as did the occupation of Nicaragua that began in 1926.

The United States invasion of Panama was authorized primarily to respond to a *domestic* American political need—the Bush Administration's feeling that it had to show the American people that it could react vigorously to provocation and that it would not allow U.S. interests to be undermined with lasting impunity.

But why an all-out *military* invasion? Couldn't an Israeli-style commando raid have achieved America's real objective in Panama—the removal of Gen. Manuel Antonio Noriega from power? The best answer appears to be that after two centuries of using the military to help conquer a continent and establish world order, nothing else seems to demonstrate resolve as emphatically to the American people.

Recall also that for more than two years the United States had tried *political* and *economic* pressure to force General Noriega to yield effective control of his country's government. Nothing worked. Then, after the Bush Administration had been highly criticized for its lack of support for a Panamanian military coup that failed in October 1989—and in contrast to a subsequent highly visible role in successfully helping to suppress an attempt to overthrow the government of the Philippines—the Administration decided that the U.S. should no longer be mocked and taunted by events in Panama. It could act on its own in dramatic fashion to preserve its self-image and the integrity of its political positions elsewhere.

Panama is Different

It must also be remembered that in the eyes of most Americans, intervening in Panama is not like intervening in any other foreign country. Panama, after all, is the site of the *Panama Canal*.

SHIP APPROACHING *one of the locks in the Panama Canal.*

The world knows the Canal as a magnificent engineering achievement. But to the people of the United States, the Canal stands as the preeminent symbol of America's reach, power, and purpose during the 20th century. They see the Canal as a boldly conceived, brilliantly executed, beneficent gift to the people of Panama that has also brought significant benefits to the United States. As such, it represents the very essence of how Americans view their country's role in the world.

Recall also that at the same time that America's position in Panama appeared to be so ineffectual, enormous political changes were occurring elsewhere in the world. The Soviet Union, China, Poland, Hungary, Czechoslovakia, East Germany, Bulgaria and Romania were each coping with radical challenges to the way their societies were controlled. As Americans watched events unfold, they realized that their country's ability to influence the course of *these* changes had been severely eroded.

Panama, however, was a different case. It was a scant 1,000 miles south of Florida; it was the site of four major U.S. bases; and it was home for more than 10,000 permanently stationed American troops. Here America could act in a way that would remind the world of its continuing importance. Moreover, separating the Panama Canal from the Republic of Panama, in the minds of most Americans, has never been easy. While many recognize the difference between the two *intellectually*, most still treat them as one entity *emotionally*. Thus, anything that troubled Panama seemed to most Americans automatically to threaten the Canal—and any threat to the Canal would be seen as a significant challenge to America's role in the world.

By moving on its own to change the way Panama was governed, America appeared to be showing *itself* that it still counted in the world. Because of the special fundamental relationship that had come to exist between the

United States and Panama—created in part by the use of the U.S. dollar as Panama's currency and by America's management of the Canal—that unilateral move appeared to have almost a *familial* aspect to it.

The invasion very much seemed as if a rich, but frustrated, *mature parent* had finally chosen to solve an embarrassing problem for its indigent and confused *adult child*.

U.S./Panamanian Relations Before World War II

The mature parent/adult child analogy serves to explain other elements in U.S./Panamanian relations over the years. For example:

- Panama was a cultural orphan almost as soon as Latin America achieved its independence from Spain in the 1820s. While geologically part of Central America, it was politically attached to South America. Yet *geographically* it was isolated from both. The fact that Americans soon began crossing the Isthmus in large numbers gave Panamanians an important alternate cultural model—one quite different from the model provided sporadically by their Hispanic realtives and neighbors.

- When gold was discovered in California in 1849, Panama became the fastest way to get from one coast to the other. Tens of thousands of travelers arrived in Panama by ship, then crossed the Isthmus by boat, mule, and on foot. Seeing this burgeoning traffic, three American entrepreneurs sought and received permission from the Colombian government (Panama was part of Colombia at the time) to build a railroad between Colon and Panama City. It opened in 1857; its successor line still operates today.

- Ferdinand de Lesseps, having successfully built the Suez Canal in Egypt, thought that he could duplicate his triumph across Panama. Despite an enormous effort, he was defeated by a debilitating climate, inadequate financing, and what proved to be a flawed engineering concept. In 1903, after intense political maneuvering among several different countries, the administration of Theodore Roosevelt took

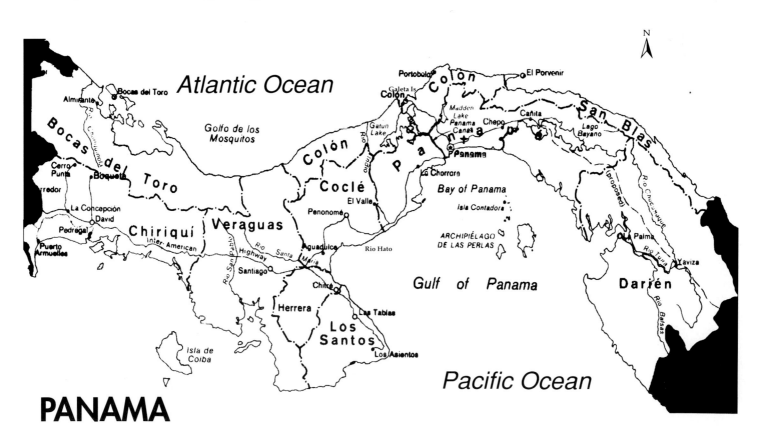

PANAMA

advantage of circumstances that gave Panama its independence and the American government an opportunity to succeed to the French excavations.

- To get a waterway completed, the Americans approached the problems presented by the Isthmus differently. First of all, the Americans decided to create a lock canal rather than the sea level canal favored

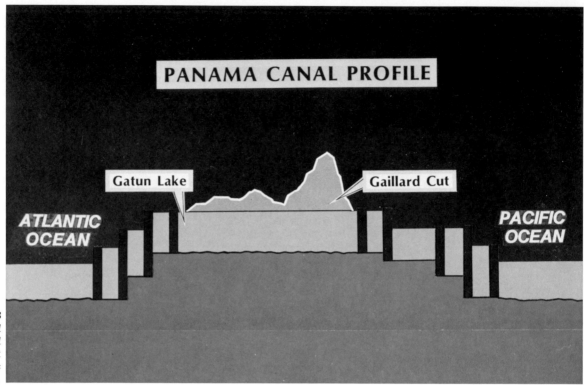

PANAMA CANAL PROFILE

Gatun Lake — Gaillard Cut

ATLANTIC OCEAN — PACIFIC OCEAN

SHIPS must be raised and lowered eighty-three feet to cross the Isthmus.

by the French. A lock canal requires ships to be mechanically lifted and lowered over an intervening barrier; a sea level canal permits ships to move between two points unimpeded once the barrier is eliminated. While sea level canals can be operationally more efficient, the mountains across the Isthmus proved too difficult to remove. Second, the Americans realized that diseases endemic to the area had to be conquered if the huge imported work force needed for the project was to survive. Once the mosquito had been identified as the carrier of yellow fever, a great tropical killer was brought under control. Third, the Americans saw the excavations required by the Canal as more of a *logistical* hurdle than an *engineering* problem. The issue for them was finding a way to remove and dispose of the dirt in a consistent, orderly, and efficient manner. Finally, the Americans determined that building the Canal would be a governmental responsibility, rather than a private undertaking. As such, the Americans could devote less energy to obtaining financing than had been the case for the French. Almost as significantly, the job of actual construction was eventually given to the U.S. Army Corps of Engineers. The Corps provided the U.S. *military* a dominant presence in Panama from the outset of the Republic's second period of independence.

- When the Canal was opened in August 1914, it became a source of tremendous national pride to all Americans. Their collective skill and treasure had accomplished what man had only been able to think about for 500 years. Once built, the Canal was also managed by Americans employed by the Department of the Army. While Panamanians did not object to the continuing American role in the *operation* of the Canal, they soon became very concerned with the U.S. government's decision to control all the ancillary *services* associated with the needs of ships transiting the Canal. These were the kinds of services that Panamanians had traditionally provided and expected to provide once the Canal was opened.

- As a result, efforts were quickly under way to clarify the treaty that had accorded the United States its original rights in Panama. In the eyes of Panamanians, the Hay/Buneau-Varilla Treaty had never been intended to allow the United States to interpret *unilaterally* what could or could not be done within the zone of land awarded to the United States. Panamanian grievances were soon numerous. Although many of them were economic in nature—involving everything from employment on the Canal to purchasing policy in the Zone—many of the grievances had to do with Panama's *sovereignty.*

PANAMA CITY in the 1930s.

Americans collected the garbage of Panama and Colon and intervened often to police the cities. America ran extensive military operations in the Zone that had little or nothing to do with directly protecting the waterway. Americans controlled the country's original international air transportation and communications linkages and even determined how and when Panamanians could cross from one end of their country to the other.

- For the most part, before World War II the grievances experienced by Panamanians were more niggling than debilitating. For every wrong that Panamanians felt they endured, there was usually some offsetting advantage—to one Panamanian group or another—that America's presence yielded. Because the original treaty gave the United States power to act in the Zone "as if it were sovereign," it did not hesitate to exercise those powers. When changes did occur, they were generally those that America decided to accord to Panama, not ones wrested by an equal political power. To some, it seemed no different than the additional privileges a parent might grant to a child as it was growing up.

- With the advent of World War II, life in Panama changed dramatically. Enormous numbers of new American troops arrived. The easy relationship and economic accommodations that had developed between U.S. officials in the Zone and the Panamanian establishment stiffened, as inexperience and uncertainty governed the actions of the newly arrived Americans. Now many of the grievances of the past found new support within Panama's political elite. American actions began to look like insults; Panamanian dignity was threatened.

U.S./Panamanian Relations After World War II

After the events of World War II, Panamanians seemed to achieve their symbolic adulthood. They could finally start to separate their admiration for American *products, services, and culture* from their distrust of U.S. *government motives, personnel, and policies.* Panamanians began seeking changes in their relationship with the United States that would demonstrate to the world that they were indeed an independent, sovereign country. But for reasons touching on the high level of domestic political power achieved by the relatively few Americans resident in the Zone, various American administrations did not want to have Panamanian sovereignty carried to the point of endangering U.S. privileges in Panama. Then a student-organized confrontation over which nation's flag should fly over the Panama Canal Zone's Balboa High School ended in several deaths. *(See photo with sign, p. 35.)* That incident convinced President Lyndon Johnson and each of his successors through Jimmy Carter that negotiations to change the *fundamental* relationship between the United States and Panama was necessary. But the change didn't come easily.

Americans at home felt that Panamanians ought to show continuing gratitude to the United States for building the Canal through their country; Americans in the Zone did not want to give up their extraordinary privileges and special way of life.

But conditions had changed over the fifty years since the Canal was opened. Panama was taking an increasingly important role in international banking and communications. The Canal had started to become less important to the U.S. military, American commercial interests, and the Panamanian economy itself. Nevertheless, it took more than thirteen years of intense discussions, active lobbying, and detailed negotiations to rescind the Hay/Buneau-Varilla Treaty of 1903 and substitute the Torrijos/Carter Treaty of 1977 (as it is known in Panama) in its stead.

Many Americans still consider the 1977 treaty (called the Panama Canal Treaty in the United States) to be wrong. They particularly oppose the heart of the agreement that specifies that ownership and control of the Canal is to pass to Panama at the end of 1999. Those Ameri-

U.S. AND PANAMANIAN FLAGS flying side by side in the Panama Canal.

cans do not believe that something that the United States built, paid for, and owns should just be *given* away. They also are concerned that Panamanians will be incapable of properly protecting and caring for it in the future.

An equal number of Panamanians, however, believe that achieving full control over the Canal symbolizes a return to the role Panama played in the world *before* the waterway was built. Those Panamanians note that the Isthmus has been used as a means of transporting goods and communicating ideas since the days of the Mayas and Incas; that Panama became the most important transit point in the world when the Spaniards used mule trains to carry colonial treasure across the Isthmus in exchange for European manufactured goods. The fundamental role of the Isthmus, they say, has not changed in five hundred years; the Canal is only an *extension* of that role. They point out that it won't be the last use of the Isthmus for the same purpose. Already, pipelines carry material that used to have to pass through the Canal on ships. In addition, ideas for a massive conveyor system and smart highways to transport containerized cargo between the two oceans have been under active study.

STATUE HONORING Torrijos/Carter Treaty of 1977.

The Invasion

How future relations between the United States and Panama may evolve is best left to a future study. For now, the concern of this book is a review of the events surrounding the destruction of the Noriega regime. We present our description in terms of the four objectives announced by the United States when it initiated its action—primarily because these four objectives seem to summarize how many American had viewed the Panamanian problem during the escalating crisis points of the previous thirty months.

For them, America's involvement in Panama has been a matter of:

- Protecting American lives;

- Enforcing the Panama Canal Treaties;

- Restoring the democratic process; and

- Bringing General Noriega to justice.

How the Bush Administration dealt with each of these objectives, how the military executed the mission given them, and how Panamanians of different political persuasions reacted to the U.S. action—originally and subsequently—is portrayed and discussed in the sections that follow. The Epilogue reviews key elements of the military operation and places the results in the context of other military actions of the past quarter century. In discussing the invasion from these different angles, we have tried to provide a comprehensive look at the broad political, economic, social, and military implications of a single event.

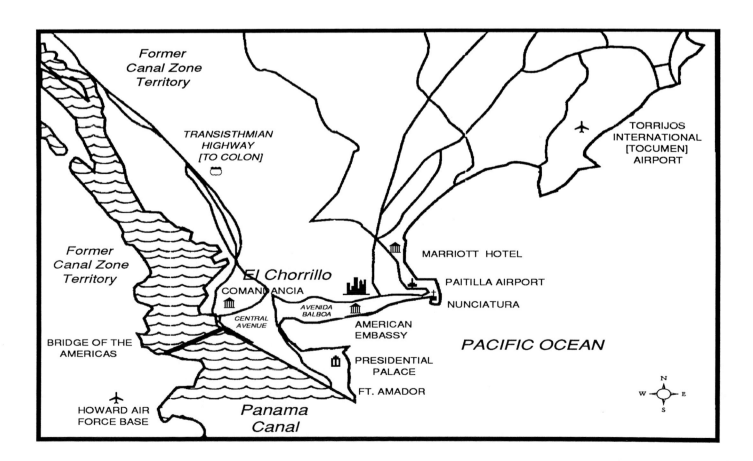

U.S. ARMY SOLDIER *guards his defense sector from a machine gun post outside of Colon.*

PROTECTING AMERICAN LIVES

AMERICAN TROOPS on patrol the morning after the invasion.

Just after one o'clock in the morning of December 20, 1989, Presidential spokesman Marlin Fitzwater entered the White House Briefing Room to announce that U.S. military forces had begun an invasion of Panama. He said that the President had ordered the action to accomplish four objectives. The *first* of these involved the protection of American lives.

No President, of course, could ignore the fact that 40,000 Americans—about three percent of Panama's urban population and one of the principal concentrations of overseas Americans anywhere—were living in and around Panama City and could eventually be threatened by General Noriega.

Included in this number were:

13,000	Regular U.S. military forces attached to the Southern Command and primarily responsible for U.S. defense interests in Latin America.
7,500	Additional troops sent into Panama over the previous thirty months to reinforce the Southern Command's standing forces defensive capabilities.
7,000	Dependents of U.S. military personnel remaining in Panama, as well as other American officials and dependents assigned to civilian government agencies operating in Panama.
3,000	American citizens and dependents still involved in the operation of the Panama Canal.
10,000	Other American citizens working in Panama or living in the country in retirement.

The problem with the Presidential statement that the United States was sending its forces into Panama *primarily* to protect American lives was that most Americans were generally not in any danger from Panamanians or from the Noriega regime *before* the invasion.

Critical Mass Reached

Americans have always felt comfortable on the Isthmus. This was true even after Panama's legislature had declared that U.S. actions to deny Panamanian-registered ships access to American ports—something that the Bush Administration had announced in November 1989—was "tantamount to a state of war." Most Americans at home, of course, didn't hear the qualifying word "tantamount"; they heard only what sounded like a formal declaration of war—something that the United States had not experienced since 1941. Even though the State Department dismissed the declaration and the legislature's election of General Noriega as the country's "Maximum Leader" as the stuff of comic operas, the subsequent death of an American military officer changed everything.

With that shooting the critical mass of political impatience with the situation in Panama had been reached. After all, eight American soldiers had died in military training accidents and other security incidents since the crisis in U.S./Panamanian relations had erupted in June 1987. Yet relatively little had been made of those unfortunate deaths—either by the Reagan Administration or by the U.S. press. But when Marine lst Lt. Robert Paz was shot, something snapped; the American people suddenly seemed to have had enough of General Noriega and what they saw as his mocking grin.

As a result, serious questions about some of the details of the incident were never raised in the U.S. media—before *or* after the invasion. No one ever gave any credence to the Panamanian explanation that Paz, by continuing to drive up a blockaded street in front of General Noriega's principal military headquarters, could have been legitimately perceived as a threat to the General's security. No one acknowledged that gunfire would surely have also erupted in *Washington, DC,* if some Spanish-speaking men had similarly decided to defy U.S. police and driven through West Executive Avenue—the blockaded street that separates the two main White House office complexes!

PELTING RAIN in Panama made soldiering tough, but it is the stuff that keeps the Panama Canal flowing.

But once opinion in America had reached the point that to do *nothing* in Panama was politically far worse than to do *something*, Washington was not inclined to start an exhaustive investigation to reach the truth about the ultimate cause of the Paz incident at the Comandancia in Panama City.

That incident—along with the subsequent bullying of a U.S. Navy lieutenant and what was labeled as the sexual harassment of his wife—gave the administration a reasonable justification to authorize a military operation that had been intensively planned for the previous three months.

The Panamanian Defense Forces (PDF)

Once the American forces began their attack, the strategy adopted to protect American lives was based on an all out effort to suppress opposition from the Panamanian Defense Forces—the PDF. This surprised some American commentators because they remembered President Bush's oft-replayed statement that the United States had no quarrel with the PDF itself, just with its commander. While some of these commentators may have expected the PDF to take the United States at its word and support the invading American forces, it would have been unrealistic to plan on it. In fact, when the shooting began, the PDF did what any military force would be expected to do: they defended themselves and their positions against unauthorized intruders.

As it turned out, then, almost the only American lives requiring protection in Panama were those of the U.S. soldiers who came to Panama to fight the Panamanian Defense Forces.

The PDF, like the Israeli Defense Force after which they were named and modeled, had a heavy concentration of personnel involved in non-military activities. The vast majority of the force was concerned with activities such as crime prevention, traffic control, ports and harbor management, customs and immigration regulation, foreign intelligence, and internal security.

The PDF had begun as a police force. For years, its highest ranking officer was a colonel. In fact, this colonel and his immediate staff tended to be members of the country's top ranking political and economic families. Over the years, though, the disparity between the relatively few families who held both political power and had financial resources—and those who did not—became even more pronounced.

BODY LANGUAGE *of U.S. soldier suggests what he thinks of a PDF Batallion motto: "The Tough Man of the Mountain Lives for War."*

The 1968 revolution in Panama, started by a relatively low ranking lieutenant colonel in the National Guard named Omar Torrijos, was designed to sever control of the country's *political* institutions from its *economic* machinery. It worked. Torrijos was able to broaden the country's political spectrum and change many long-held Panamanian attitudes about the proper involvement of government in social matters. At the same time that Torrijos was reducing the elite's political power, he was providing attractive incentives for them to build a stronger economy. While they had lost much of their political influence, many soon found themselves making even more money than before.

Torrijos also realized that both sectors had to have a common goal if the changes he sought were to be lasting. He saw control of the Panama Canal and the territory that surrounded it as the most obvious issue to engender pride among all Panamanians. After years of negotiation, Torrijos won a new Panama Canal Treaty from the United States and encouraged Panamanians to ratify its terms.

In 1981, General Omar Torrijos died in a plane crash. Two years later, he was succeeded by Manuel Antonio Noriega. The separation of political and economic power no longer made sense to General Noriega and his colleagues. Those who had achieved *political* power began looking for ways to increase their *economic* standing. The expansion of the National Guard into the Panamanian Defense Forces opened new avenues for economic gain. Once the possibilities of using governmental positions to acquire significant wealth became obvious, the boundaries of law and propriety were often overcome by greed. When the level of corruption and interference began to erode the economic power of the elite—in effect reversing the Torrijos Revolution—opposition to the Noriega regime eventually manifested itself—with substantial U.S. encouragement—in the form of a united political organization that came to be called the Civic Crusade. *(See photo on p. 89.)*

Because so many of the PDF were involved with non-military activities, the United States faced only about 6,000 combat-ready Panamanian soldiers. They were really no match for the U.S. Army, Navy, and Air Force. In terms of numbers, tactics, and equipment, U.S. superiority was quickly established. The war to conquer the PDF was a short one. It was over in about five hours. In the process, however, the punishment both sides suffered turned out to be serious:

23	American soldiers died.
3	American civilians lost their lives.
50	Panamanian Defense Force personnel died—according to the Pentagon's revised estimate. *(The original count was 314.)*
1,000+	Panamanian civilians estimated to have lost their lives in the invasion. *(The Pentagon originally said there were 202 civilian deaths, but later acknowledged the inaccuracy of that count. A private U.S. group documents 302 civilians who died. Panamanians themselves believe many more than 500 died, with some estimates as high as 5,000 deaths.)*

PANAMANIAN AND U.S. FLAGS *outside the American Embassy in Panama.*

In addition, some 324 Americans and at least 3,000 Panamanians were wounded during Operation Just Cause.

It should be noted that *Panamanian deaths* —given Panama's 2.4 million population—were equivalent to more than *twice* the number that the United States lost in the entire Viet Nam War. The actual price paid by Panama for its liberation from General Noriega's domination, then, was an extraordinarily high one.

The Dignity Battalions

Once the invasion had been *launched*, American lives were certainly put in danger. While the PDF had been defeated, members of the Noriega regime's Dignity Battalions were still at large. The Dignity Battalions had been formed as a home guard in 1988 when the threat of U.S. military action then seemed possible. At the beginning, they were treated as little more than a human shield—an essentially untrained, lightly armed, paramilitary force to be thrust in front of U.S. forces should they decide to invade. After a while, though, the Dignity Battalions took on a life of their own. Membership in the Battalions not only provided a source of income to people who otherwise would have been unemployed in a heavily depressed economy, but it conveyed a measure of status to its members as well. In addition, General Noriega's people found a *domestic* use for the Battalions: they would serve as civilian defenders of the regime against the organized political opposition. Unfortunately, the ranks of the Dignity Battalions became riddled with ordinary thugs and common criminals who vented their larger hatreds, prejudices, and frustrations in vicious attacks on fellow Panamanians.

Once the PDF had essentially collapsed as a fighting force around dawn on December 20, 1989, the Dignity Battalions disintegrated as organized units as well. Whether by design or by circumstance, individual members of the Battalions began roaming the streets, sniping at U.S. forces, endangering American and Panamanian civilians, setting fires to buildings, and looting some stores. The United States had severely underestimated the danger from the "Dingbats" (as some Americans began calling them.) As a result, the threat to isolated Americans in the first 12 hours of the invasion increased markedly.

Three groups of Americans were in the most danger: those at the Smithsonian Research Station on Galeta Island, those at the U.S. Embassy, and those at the Marriott Hotel. The Smithsonian scientists were taken

LAURA BROOKS of NBC radio (center) covers a U.S. Southern Command press briefing.

into custody by PDF troops, but were soon released. The Embassy was secured after some fairly nervous hours and only after someone called Washington directly to ask that the Southern Command be *ordered* to protect the compound. The Marriott was liberated the next day after Panamanian forces arrived to take hostages. The U.S. media, most of whom were staying at the Marriott, reported their exposure and lack of protection on U.S. radio and television. A lot of America—and all of Washington—heard their complaint, could appreciate their terror, and demanded a response. It eventually came with a rush of armor, personnel, and electronic equipment.

This invasion, after all, was not a pure military operation. It was also an exercise to prove to the American people that the United States could still enforce its will when required.

As such, it would have been extraordinarily embarrassing to have a repeat of the Tehran hostage situation and it would have been worse to have the U.S. press—most of whom arrived *after* an invasion said to be primarily intended to protect American lives—end up in danger of losing theirs. In fact, the domestic public relations aspects of the invasion always seemed evident. Why else would the United States send its sophisticated Air Force F-117A stealth *fighter* on a mission from California to engage Panamanian defenses? As far as anyone knew, Panama's air defenses were rudimentary at best. One reasonable explanation offered was that the Pentagon had an interest in demonstating stealth technology to improve the chances of funding the still-pending production version of the B-2 stealth *bomber*.

Despite the casualties eventually suffered, despite some genuinely scary moments, and despite the few mistakes committed, no one doubted that in the end the U.S. military had demonstrated that it could perform its first mission—protecting American lives—in exemplary fashion.

PDF HEADQUARTERS burns in the early morning hours after the invasion was launched. Note the helicopter observing from above.

SOLDIER *cautiously approaches a heavily shelled PDF building .*

ON PATROL *through the rubble-strewn streets of El Chorrillo.*

APC ASSUMES DEFENSIVE POSITION *in the doorway of a laundry.*

ON THE JOB IN PANAMA *(This page clockwise from top right):* **SOLDIER APPLYING CAMOUFLAGE** *paint before patrol.* **PERSPIRING OFFICERS** *attending a news conference inside an air conditioned hotel.* **METEOROLOGIST CHECKING DATA** *for the Canal area.*
THE COLON TO PANAMA *road in the footsteps of Balboa, Drake, Morgan, the 49ers, and others.*

(This page clockwise from top left: **ARMORED COLUMN** *near the American Embassy on Avenida Balboa.* **DETAINEES** *behind barbed wire.* **ARMY CONSTRUCTION CREWS** *clearing away destruction debris.* **MOVIE BREAK** *for off-duty invasion troops— with parental guidance still recommended for both films.*

BUILDING overlooking a school playground is destroyed in the aftermath of the invasion.

COLON WAREHOUSE proved to be a major weapons storage facility. Despite sign, building was never used as a children's day care center.

SIGN on headquarters of Panama's FBI equivalent (DENI) honors those who died in 1964 clash with U.S. military. It states: "For Panama Our Lives" and commands Panamanians: "Not One Step Back."

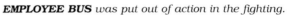

REPAIRING THE DAMAGE to buildings at Ft. Amador, a shared U.S./ Panamanian facility. No one is certain how long it will take the palm tree to recover from the shelling it received.

EMPLOYEE BUS was put out of action in the fighting.

AIR POWER—*to support combat operations, provide supplies, and conduct reconnaissance—was concentrated at Howard Air Force Base.*

CREW MEMBERS
*conferring outside a
Blackhawk helicopter.*

HELICOPTER
*crossing
Panama Bay.*

MILITARY AIRLIFT COMMAND *personnel
unloading a helicopter in Panama.*

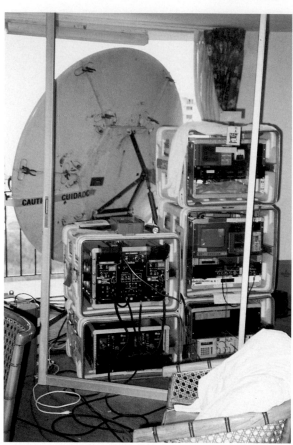

SATELLITE DISH *erected on a hotel balcony helped get the story of the invasion to worldwide television viewers.*

MEDIA CENTER *was quickly created in Holiday Inn by televisian technicians.*

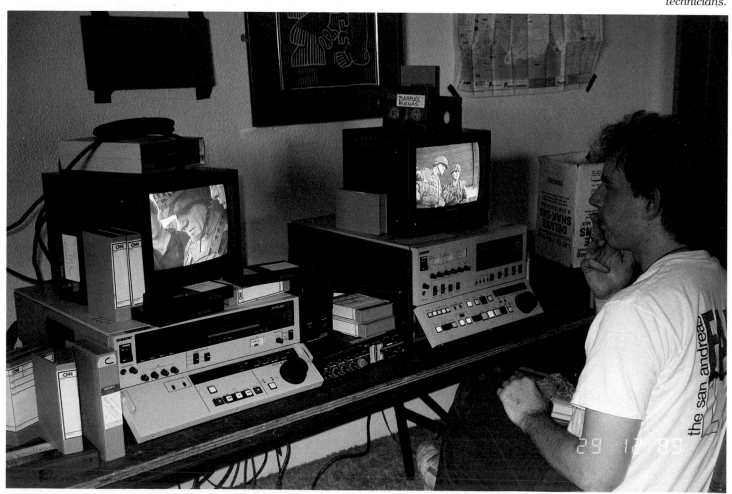

38

**CNN'S
CHARLES JACO**
*reporting from the
18th floor of the
Holiday Inn.*

SOLDIER USES KEVLAR HELMET *as billboard to proclaim his feelings during holiday invasion.*

GENERAL COLIN L. POWELL, *Chairman of the Joint Chiefs of Staff, dealing with the media on his post-invasion visit to Panama.*

GENERAL MAXWELL R. THURMAN, *Commander-in-Chief of the U.S. Southern Command, hurrying into a press conference.*

LIEUTENANT GENERAL CARL W. STINER, *operational commander for the invasion, answering NBC radio reporter Ross W. Simpson's questions.*

**PHOTOGRAPHS OF
CAPTURED WEAPONS**
*displayed for visiting
dignitaries.*

SENATORS ROBB, NUNN, AND WARNER
*(left to right) flanked
by military escorts during
their post-invasion tour.*

GENERAL MANUEL NORIEGA'S ENGRAVED PISTOL
*along with hundreds of other pistols, stacked rifles, and
assorted weapons captured or confiscated
during the invasion.*

MAKESHIFT MP MOTOR POOL
for Humvees (the Jeep's replacement)
is created in one of Panama City's
older neighborhoods.

SHIPS APPROACHING the Atlantic entrance of the Panama Canal.

ENFORCING THE PANAMA CANAL TREATIES

At the time of the U.S. invasion, the Panama Canal had been operating continuously under American management for more than seventy-five years. The fact that it had *never* closed for any reason was amazing, particularly in light of two world wars and numerous regional conflicts, political crises, labor disputes, police actions, weather problems, and mechanical difficulties.

It is ironic, then, that the only closure ever experienced by the Canal was at the time of —and solely because of —a *United States* invasion of Panama, rather than as the result of some external or third power threat.

BRIDGE OF THE AMERICAS *(formerly known as the Thatcher Ferry Bridge) spans the Pacific entrance of the Canal.*

U.S. Rights

As part of America's justification for the invasion, President Bush cited the need to enforce the 1977 Panama Canal Treaties. One of those treaties had been clarified in the Senatorial ratification process to ensure that there was no doubt that the President of the United States had the right to "protect and defend" the Canal whenever its security was threatened. The military officers to whom the President had delegated this responsibility determined that the best way to protect and defend the Canal, in the wake of the invasion, was to *close* it. This proved totally unnecessary.

No information of any kind about a threat to the Canal—before, during, or since the invasion—has ever surfaced. Those who maintained guard around the locks and patrolled parts of the waterway after the invasion saw no action. It may well be that those who decided on closure were not aware of the proud, unbroken—and politically impartial—record of continuous Canal service. It is much more likely, however, that the decision to close the Canal was seen as a prudent *military* tactic—insuring a "clear field of fire" to U.S. forces in the event of problems.

U.S. NAVAL VESSELS *patrolling the Panama Canal at the outset of the invasion.*

Some observers might have thought that closing the Canal would have created a negative reaction in many other countries. If it did, it was lost in the overwhelmingly positive public reaction that the Canal's *reopening* generated. When the Canal was once again declared safe for inter-ocean traffic, it was taken as a dramatic signal that one of the primary U.S. objectives for the invasion had already been achieved with American lives still threatened and General Noriega still at large. Every news brief reporting on the invasion proclaimed that the Canal was back in business; none bothered to note that it had never before been out of business nor that it had been in no danger in the first place.

While it is demonstrably true that the Canal's ancient lock mechanisms are vulnerable to various techniques of modern terrorism, Panamanians themselves have always been extremely protective of the Canal. It not only helps define their country, but it has been an important source of income as well.

The Canal's Significance

As every Panamanian knows and many like to point out—but some Americans have never fully appreciated—the Canal is much more important to Panama than it is to the United States.

When the Canal first came into operation, it had no real competition. Shipping goods *through* the Canal saved considerable time and money; the only alternative was sending material around Cape Horn. But about the mid-1970s, pipeline technology and containerization techniques made the cost of transportation *across* the United States competitive with the time and expense involved in transiting the Canal. As a result, long term closure of the Canal would reinforce the competitive position of the United States in inter-oceanic transportation systems—something the people of Panama would be loathe to do.

The reason is not connected with preserving trade patterns for the time when Panama assumes responsibility for the Canal in 1999. Rather, Panamanians are conscious of the *ancillary* commercial activity that the Canal now generates for Panama. The Canal, after all, reinforced the importance of the country's central geographical position in the Western Hemisphere. The Canal created a foundation for Panama's dollar-based economy, offering price stability absent in many other surrounding countries. The Canal provided many Panamanians with an internationally beneficial fluency in the English language—not only because of the large American presence in the country and not only due to the Panamanians studying in the United States, but also because of the numerous Panamanians descended from native English speakers brought in from Caribbean islands for the construction of the Canal. Finally, the Canal demanded a sophisticated communication system and supporting transportation network (highways, airlines, railroads, pipelines)—which in turn were important in attracting non-transportation businesses to the country. Taken together, all of these Canal-related advantages have resulted in the following:

- Panama had become one of the world's leading international banking centers before the crisis with the U.S. began; more than ninety-five foreign banks still do business there. While about a dozen banks were forced to abandon their Panamanian activities during the economic crisis created by U.S. sanctions directed against the Noriega regime and total bank employment dropped significantly, this sector of the Panamanian economy has become too important to world commerce to remain depressed for long. *(See related photo, p. 60.)*

- The Colon Free Zone has now grown to become the third largest specialized trading area in the world. Goods manufactured all over the world are shipped to Panama—where they are put on display in what amounts to a perpetual Latin American trade fair, assembled into finished products, or merely held in storage pending further distribution. The Colon Free Zone accounts for nearly $5 billion in annual sales and employs thousands of Panamanians; its activities survived the political crisis and invasion in reasonably sound condition. *(See photo, p. 55)*

- Panama has developed an important business support industry—serving as one of the world's principal locations for centralizing multi-national corporate activities and becoming the country of record for the second largest fleet of merchant ships in the world. This in turn has spawned an active hospitality industry, manifested by large hotels, several duty free shopping areas, and important tourist facilities and attractions.

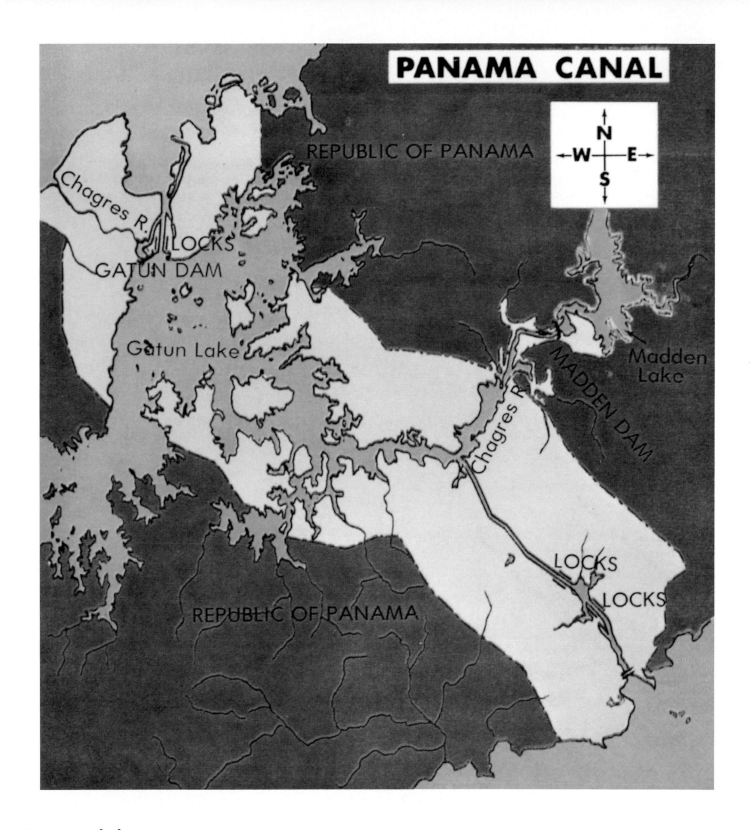

PANAMA CANAL

Commercial Chaos

But the United States objective of enforcing the 1977 Panama Canal Treaties—and all that those treaties implied for America's historic role in Panama and Panama's own economy—also harmed the economy. As soon as America's overwhelming military power was targeted on the PDF, the institution collapsed. When the command and control structure of the PDF disintegrated, the nation's police functions also failed. With no organized force available to guard *Panamanian* property during the invasion, scores of past grudges and pent-up deprivation were settled in a fit of destruction and looting. Shop owners and managers able to get to their businesses before the mobs responded by mounting their own round-the-clock armed protection.

While the thought of an armed *civilian* effort to get rid of General Noriega never arose, an armed response to the looting was instantaneous. This surprised some who had come to think of Panamanians as an inherently docile people. Yet it was a typically Panamanian reaction to an intensely *personal* problem.

The invasion demonstrated that Panamanians are, by heritage and by circumstance, more oriented to commerce than to politics. Mess with their government and they may shrug; mess with their livelihoods and they become intensely involved. It is an interesting lesson for the future.

FREIGHTER being escorted through the Canal under the watchful eyes of an American machine gunner.

SIGNS *in any language had no impact on looters in the chaos generated by the invasion.*

TRASHED CARTONS AND WRAPPING MATERIAL *heaped outside of a looted warehouse near the Colon Free Zone.*

CENTRAL AVENUE, *Panama's famed principal shopping district, littered with trash on the day before Christmas.*

24 12 89

56

FRONT-END LOADERS *had to be used to clear some streets of debris left by looters.*

EVEN THE MANNEQUIN *(foreground) was dismembered in the looting.*

TELEVISION CREW *films and records*

STORE'S LIGHTS *illuminate devastation rather than merchandise.*

a stunned store owner.

HUGE SALE *proclaimed by sign turned into grand loot.*

EMPTY SHELVES *is all that remains of the crystal department in this store.*

AUTOMATIC TELLER MACHINE (ATM)
*looks like a can pried open with a knife
after looters finished removing money in
holding container.*

DISEMBOWELED Texaco gasoline pump is stark evidence that virtually nothing unprotected escaped destruction or looting.

SIGN ANNOUNCES A TOTAL CLEARANCE SALE. *Store owners got their wish, but no money changed hands.*

PAWNSHOP'S HEAVY GRATING *made no difference to looters intent on getting at jewelry and other items inside this store.*

YOUNG BOY *scurries down Central Avenue with loot clutched firmly in his hand.*

BICYCLE TIRES—*neatly tied together for easier handling—are calmly rolled out of this bicycle shop.*

WHATEVER WAS LEFT IN THE TRASH *seems of value to these boys.*

ENTERPRISING CUNA INDIAN FAMILY *acquired a dolly to remove looted goods.*

IRONING BOARD, SOFA, *and other large pieces had to be transported home in trucks— some of which were stolen for the task.*

CHRISTMAS FRUIT CAKES *went on sale on the street moments after being looted from a store.*

SHOESHINE MAN stoically maintains his stand next to a looted shop.

AMERICAN SOLDIER, *in a classic close-the-barn-door-after-the-horse-has-escaped gesture, is posted in a doorway long after looters had emptied the store of anything worth safeguarding.*

PANAMA'S PRESIDENTIAL PALACE

Because Panama has never had much of a democratic tradition, it was somewhat surprising for the President of the United States to cite the *restoration* of the democratic process as one of America's objectives for the invasion.

Perhaps the use of the term "restoration" was merely a mistaken choice of words, not some fundamental misreading of Panamanian history. Technically, it is hard to restore something that may never have existed in the first place. After all, the U.S. said nothing when it realized that the Noriega regime had manipulated the 1984 presidential vote count to ensure the election of Nicolás Ardito Barletta, a talented economist and former student of then Secretary of State George Schultz. In addition, of course, since the earliest days of its independence, Panama has been controlled by one homogeneous group or another. Instead of spirited competition *among* contending economic and social groups to establish a specific set of political values, Panamanian politics have generally been characterized by contests between "ins" and "outs" of the *same* group. Moreover, the *outs* have tended to get *in* through the use of armed force rather than as the result of democratic processes.

Democracy's Appeal

Perhaps the reference to democracy was just a sign of the times. After all, the events sweeping the world in 1989 evoked enormously powerful images—of unhappy citizens visibly expressing their pent-up impatience with the inadequacies of their authoritarian systems and demanding that a more responsive system replace them. But those powerful moments of people going into the streets calling for democracy failed to generate any demonstrable official U.S. enthusiasm; for whatever reason, the American administration stood mostly mute in the face of the dramatic events abroad—an observer, not even a cheerleader.

But once the Bush Administration had at last determined how it wanted to resolve the Panamanian situation, it also saw an opportunity to demonstrate a strong commitment to the concept of democracy as well.

Moreover, the U.S. could make its statement about democracy without wondering how any other *government* might react. The nature of the U.S. invasion of Panama, after all, was a singular undertaking; it proceeded without asking anyone's permission—including anyone in power in Panama—and it concluded when the U.S. had decided that it had accomplished what it needed to do. In addition, invoking the idea that the U.S. invasion was designed somehow to protect aspects of the democratic ideal was good public relations. It has proven an effective trigger mechanism for public support ever since

AMERICAN AND PANAMANIAN relations take on the appearance of returning to normal.

President Woodrow Wilson justified the U.S. entrance into World War I as a way to make the world safe for democracy.

Elections and Democracy

Most Americans tend to equate democracy with elections. So long as a fair electoral process is periodically *available* to make changes in how a government operates—should the need to seek change arise—Americans usually assume that a democratic process exists.

But real democracy, of course, encompasses much more than just elections. It involves such other matters as the inviolability of basic human rights as well as freedom of expression, movement, thought, and choice. These are essentially *political* freedoms. It's not that they are unimportant to Panamanians; they are. But as was pointed out in the previous section, most Panamanians tend to relate the value of these freedoms in terms of their *economic* applicability.

Democracy in Panama

Panamanians have always had what seems to be a fairly detached view toward their own governmental system—if it didn't interfere with their ability to make a living or spend their money, few paid much attention to how it was organized or what it actually did.

This is obviously a far cry from President John F. Kennedy's famous conception of government's relationship to its citizenry. Panamanians seldom ask what their government can do for them and they generally are not interested in finding out what they can do for their government. Most Panamanians ask only that their government leave them alone.

PANAMANIAN JEWISH COMMUNITY *gathers to listen to new government's leaders.*

In a sense, the ultimate sin of the Noriega regime—in the eyes of many Panamanians—may have been that it eventually became *too* involved in Panamanian life. Some of that involvement was the result of excessive greed; some of it resulted from the impact of U.S. sanctions and the pressure they applied on the economy; and some of it was a combination of both and a fear among some Noriega supporters of losing the special privileges that government power can provide to others.

For the Bush Administration, however, the goal of *restoring* democracy to Panama really meant only one thing: seeing that Guillermo Endara, Ricardo Arias Calderon, and Guillermo Ford—the Presidential and Vice Presidential candidates that had been openly and financially backed by the United States in the May 1989 elections—were at last installed in the offices they had won.

Meaningfully, the installation of Panama's new constitutional officers occurred *before* the United States invasion had actually commenced. In one sense, then, the United States seemed to accomplish at least one of its goals without firing a shot or endangering a soldier.

But in a larger sense, of course, the U.S. still had much to do to accomplish the goal of restoring democracy. For one thing, it was days after the Endara government had been recognized by the United States that the Election Tribunal was convened to formally declare the actual winners of the presidential and vice presidential races. For another, the government lacked the financial and law enforcement resources to take full control of the country. Furthermore, no one in the U.S. government seemed concerned that the winning candidates for the national *legislature*—hotly contested races run at the same time as the presidential election—were not similarly identified and installed in office. Apparently only after Latin American governments had made the functioning of the legislature a condition for their recognition of the new government, and only after the United States sought a change in Panama's banking secrecy laws, did the focus shift to the constitutional necessity of getting the legislature back into business.

NEW PANAMANIAN POLICEMAN *stands guard without socks, weapon, or proper equipment.*

Panama's part in the democratic move-ments of 1989 matched the experiences of other countries. It was not so much that democratic processes needed to be *restored;* it was that a democratic tradition still needed to be *established.*

VEHICLES BLOCKADE STREETS *to prevent outsiders from entering a neighborhood.*

STOLEN BUS *forms a substantial roadblock. Graffiti under window translates as: "Noriega - Gay and a Coward."*

CONDOMINIUM RESIDENT *partrols building in the absence of regular police force.*

SUPERMARKET"S FRONT OFFICE PERSONNEL *take on new chores to safeguard merchandise from looters.*

MODERN VIGILANTES *at ease with their weapons in front of their stores.*

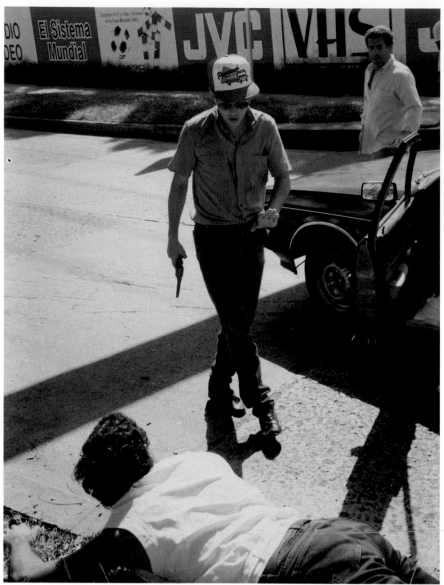

ARMED CITIZEN *forces possible looter out of car and to the street.*

SUSPECTED LOOTER is unceremoniously trussed
and left in the sun pending a decision
on what to do with the prisoner.
(He was eventually released.)

HAND-LETTERED SIGN IN POOR SPANISH READS: *"Armed Forces of the United States. If you know information or have found arms, please wait here. Do Not Enter."* Given the state of anarchy in the country, *few gave up* all *the weapons they knew about or possessed.*

SIGN PAINTED ON BED SHEET, *laid out on a street and weighted down by rocks, expresses an overwhelming Panamanian sentiment.*

PANAMANIAN PRESIDENT GUILLERMO ENDARA
smiles broadly as U.S. Vice President Dan Quayle gestures.

U.S. VICE PRESIDENT with American
troops watching 1990 Super Bowl
in Panama.

PANAMANIAN VICE PRESIDENT GUILLERMO FORD, PRESIDENT GUILLERMO ENDARA GALIMANY, AND VICE PRESIDENT RICARDO ARIAS CALDERON (left to right) acknowledge cheers in the first days of their Administration. (Note that President Endara's mother's surname—Galimany—is used in Panama.)

REFUGEE CAMP established at a
baseball stadium for some of the
12,000 who lost their homes during
the invasion. Replacement cost for the
estimated 4000 destroyed houses
may exceed $100 million.

THREE'S COMPANY
*as American soldiers
are entertained by
Panamanian children.*

PML—PERSONNEL MOVEMENT LIMITATION—*restricted travel of U.S. forces and their dependents in Panama. Panamanians paid close attention to each change in level as it was announced over the U.S. Southern Command's radio and television networks. ECHO—"no movement except for official business"—was declared only a few hours before the invasion.*

PANAMANIANS CELEBRATING
the surrender of General Noriega
to U.S. government authorities
on the night of January 3, 1990.
The bottle contains Panamanian
rum.

JOYOUS WOMAN
*stands under the flag
of the Civic Crusade—
the organization
founded in 1987
to oppose the
Noriega regime.*

BANGING ON POTS AND PANS
became the trademark form of protest for Panamanians opposed to the Noriega regime. Here some ladies recall their previous activities—but this time out of joy rather than enmity.

BMW FILLED WITH CHEERING KIDS
suggests the economic differences that separated those who originally opposed General Noriega (the wealthy) from those who tended to support him .

U.S. TROOPS *join the infectious celebrations on top of a fire truck.*

SOLDIERS TAKING A BREAK *during the Carnival atmosphere that marked the beginning of the end of their duty in Panama.*

OPERATION JUST CAUSE T-SHIRTS *sprouted all over the city just after Christmas to proclaim appreciation for the American liberation.*

HUGE CROWDS *gathered in a field along Avenida Balboa—among billboards for Btesh (a men's store), Copa (an airlines), and Nat Mendez (a jewelry store) —to demand an end to General Noriega's asylum.*

HIGH RISE TENANTS *on their balconies in support of the crowds below demanding that General Noriega leave the Nunciatura.*

BRINGING GENERAL NORIEGA TO JUSTICE

Although bringing General Noriega to justice was the last of the U.S. objectives for the invasion of Panama— and made to sound the least important of them—it was in fact the whole point of Operation Just Cause. Here again, the *actual* wording of the goal was misleading.

After all, it was General Noriega's removal from *power*, more than his being brought to *justice*, that seemed so vital to the Bush Administration and the United States.

"WE HAVE A COMMANDER FOR A LONG WHILE" notes the caption (incorrectly, as it turned out) of a photo on the wall of one of General Noriega's offices.

General Noriega's Reach in Panama

From an American military standpoint, of course, *neutralizing* General Noriega in any way possible made utmost sense. If he were to remain in Panama, he could rally surviving elements of the Panamanian Defense Forces after the initial American assault. The possibility that the United States might eventually get caught up in another Viet Nam-like, jungle-based, guerrilla war was the most harrowing political prospect of the invasion. Such lingering situations—where public attitudes can turn from interest to boredom to annoyance—bring American governments down. On the other hand, if General Noriega were to escape to a third country, he would be able to offer to the world's press tantalizing bits of information that might prove politically distressing to President Bush and/or the United States government.

As a result, fixing his precise location had been a major intelligence requirement for weeks before the invasion on December 20, 1989. It seems that just before the invasion was launched, he was moving from his Casa del Recuerdo office *(see photo, p. 103)* toward Tucumen Airport. General Noriega had expected the United States to try to kill or capture him first. He figured that a full-fledged invasion would come *only* if the attempt failed. He certainly had not anticipated that an invasion would be launched *before* a massive search for him was under way.

THE GENERAL AND MRS. NORIEGA *(Felicidad Sieiro de Noriega) at a country fair in 1989.*

While this miscalculation probably made the collapse of the PDF quicker, it also allowed General Noriega to evade U.S. authorities longer. Keeping him moving, rather than directing the PDF troops, was apparently part of the overall Panamanian strategy.

But even more than the military/political reasons associated with his apprehension, the *public relations* value of his demise was paramount. Without being able to silence him permanently, the clear and complete destruction of his regime could not be guaranteed. A Noriega at large and capable of taunting the United States would have left the American people feeling unfulfilled. Everyone in Washington understood this; and no one in authority wanted to have to justify the invasion and loss of life while trying to explain that General Noriega's capture didn't really matter. It did. General Noriega, after all, was no ordinary international villain in American eyes.

He was not only portrayed by exiled Panamanians as the leader of a criminal enterprise who ruthlessly murdered his political opponents, but he was described by the U.S. Attorney in Miami as the one person responsible for killing America's kids with drugs.

Here was an officer of the Federal judicial system determining General Noriega's *guilt* on national television. No presumption of innocence, no scrutiny of the evidence, no trial. Perhaps such niceties of American justice weren't really necessary. With General Noriega in Panama, only the court of public opinion in the U.S. was thought to be available to judge him. That court was quick to sentence him. Various commentators started referring to him as the *world's* most important narco-terrorist. No one seemed to doubt it.

General Noriega's Role in U.S. Politics

A few months later, Vice President Bush's 1988 presidential campaign ran into a problem. It needed an issue to demonstrate his political independence from Ronald Reagan. To solve the dilemma, George Bush declared that *he* would never negotiate with any drug dealing dictators. Given the intense and well-leaked official discussions then going on between the Reagan Administration and the Noriega regime, there could be no doubt that George Bush had General Noriega in mind.

Neither Panama's well-being nor U.S. international interests were involved in the Bush speech; domestic U.S. politics were. Many months later, of course, the leadership in China would be accused of directly committing far worse crimes against the youth of *their* country than General Noriega was ever said to be responsible for inside or outside of Panama. But the leadership of China would be forgiven their crimes by then *President* George Bush because of a larger goal he said he was trying to accomplish. To even suggest forgiving General Noriega for past sins after George Bush had become President would seem to undercut the integrity of Bush's anticipated *1992* reelection campaign. As a result, General Noriega was not someone George Bush wanted to do business with and he didn't.

But that attitude didn't solve the problem either. Part of the reason that the United States had so much trouble being done with General Noriega was that not everyone in the *United States* or *Panama* saw him in the same light. Many loyal Panamanians who worked for the Panamanian government during his era, for example, were part of the large political organization that supported his continuation in office. Not all of the civil servants, union members, PDF soldiers, and political functionaries that worked with General Torrijos and General Noriega over the years were corrupt, venal, or evil.

Many of them, in fact, believed in the broad goals of their political movement. They further believed that the United States had no business telling Panama how or by whom it ought to be governed. In addition, some felt that the opposition Civic Crusade had a racist streak that disqualified it from governing a multi-racial society while others thought that some members of the opposition only wanted to satisfy their own greed after the overthrow of General Noriega's regime.

General Noriega's Connection to the U.S. Government

Whatever the truth of the situation in the United States or Panama, one thing is certain: General Manuel Antonio Noriega was a complex man with an intriguing career:

- He had long claimed to have been a friend of George Bush's—even said that he hoped Bush would be elected U.S. President. The connection stemmed from the days when George Bush was in charge of the CIA and then Colonel Noriega was in charge of all intelligence activities for the Panamanian government. Although President Bush at first denied ever meeting General Noriega, a picture of them together served to refresh Mr. Bush's memory. Because of this background, the possibility that the two did intelligence business together has continually fueled speculation about what that might have involved. Some believe that Noriega knows a great deal; Bush says he doesn't know what that could be; and Noriega has not said anything as yet.

- General Noriega proved very cooperative to the U.S. Drug Enforcement Administration in its efforts to stop the flow of drugs to the United States. As a result, he earned generous letters of commendation from DEA Administrators for the effective work he and his colleagues had done. Some have suggested that the drug operations that General Noriega participated in were just a convenient way to deflect suspicion about his own *larger* illicit drug activities; other have said that people caught by General Noriega were those who refused to give him or his friends their expected share of the drug business. Again the *truth* of General Noriega's exact involvement with drug trafficking has not yet been fully determined.

- General Noriega served many other United States interests over the years. For example, he participated in the decision to send Panamanian soldiers to the Sinai as part of a United Nations Middle Eastern Peace Keeping Force the United States strongly favored. He mounted a massive operation to protect the Shah of Iran once the Shah's continued presence in the United States proved politically difficult for the Carter Administration. In addition, the United States helped General Noriega train and equip Battalion 2000, the unit that would eventually be given principal responsibility for protecting the Panama Canal. Most significantly, the Defense Department enjoyed the benefits of deploying large numbers of soldiers on four large, tranquil bases in Panama in sharp contrast to difficulties experienced by U.S. forces on overseas bases in Greece, Spain, the Philippines, Korea, the Azores and elsewhere.

- It also appears that General Noriega may have been involved in the Israeli connection to the Nicaraguan Contras. Testimony during the Iran/Contra hearings revealed the fact that the idea of selling weapons to the Iranians came originally

CHOCOE INDIANS *from the Darien region of Panama surround the General.*

from Israel; the *proceeds* from those sales, of course, eventually were used to pay Contra military expenses. The Congress, it will be recalled, had prohibited the Administration from spending on lethal supplies for the Contras. In addition, it seems that some weaponry originally in Israel's possession was diverted to the Contras *through* Panama with General Noriega's assistance. In fact, there is some thought that General Noriega's problems with the United States actually started in 1985 when he refused to help the United States establish a second, southern front for the Contras.

- Because of the money that General Noriega was said to have received from the CIA and other U.S. agencies, his dealings over the years with Cuba's Fidel Castro, his friendship with Nicaragua's Daniel Ortega, and his loan arrangements with Libya's Moammar Qaddafi have all raised interesting questions about whether those connections actually *served* or *hindered* the interests of the United States—or might have done both at the same time for different U.S. agencies.

The multi-faceted relationship between General Noriega and the United States over the past twenty years has fueled a massive amount of speculation as to what he knows and what he may do with the information in the future.

General Noriega's Experience with the Papal Nuncio

The public may never be party to the answers. In fact, the smart money had always assumed that General Noriega would never be brought to the United States alive; these analysts held that the United States really didn't want to have to deal with any information he may reveal in open court; that to deny his right to present evidence about his dealings with the U.S. government might force his release which would be worse than not bringing him to trial in the first place. It was for this reason, particularly, that his sudden appearance at the Papal Nuncio's residence on Christmas Eve caused such a sensation.

THE NUNCIATURA as seen from the front gate. Note the two towers behind the Papal diplomatic mission. The one to the left is a condominium while the round tower to the right is the Holiday Inn.

In the four days that he remained at large in Panama, the search for him dominated the press. With a $1 million reward for information about him, with Panamanians looking for him, and with all of the U.S. forces trying to find him, it seemed impossible that he could elude the net set for him or that he would emerge alive. His hope from the outset was to hold out pending an international demand for the United States to leave Panama. When the resolution of the Organization of American States on the invasion proved weak (it only expressed "deep regret") and the United Nations postponed debate for a week, the General and his people discussed continuing the fight in the hills.

Former Minister of Commerce and Industry Mario Rognoni asked Noriega if the PDF was organized for a guerrilla war. The response was that they were, but the batteries to their portable radios had died. "Then we aren't really organized," said Rognoni. It was at this point that Noriega accepted the fact that further resistance would be too costly. He and his close advisors decided to head for the sanctuary of various embassies. When General Noriega successfully reached the Papal Nuncio's residence in the Nuncio's own limousine (perhaps with the silent complicity of the United States *Army* in the interest of putting an end to the fighting), an entirely new headache was created for the United States *government.*

But why the Papal Nuncio's residence instead of the Cuban, Nicaraguan, or Libyan embassies? The story has to return to May 1988 when the United States and Panama were very close to resolving the crisis in their relations. The Papal Nuncio, Juan Laboa, had been involved in those discussions. When the negotiations eventually collapsed, Laboa knew that the United States had been primarily responsible for ending them, not General Noriega as Secretary of State George Schultz told a press conference. General Noriega, of course, knew this background and sought refuge in the Nuncio's residence because of the kindred spirit he assumed he would find there.

It now appears that General Noriega eventually decided to turn himself over to the United States government, rather than go down fighting as some thought he might, because he was finally convinced that the truth about his dealings with the United States needed to be told. Some who know him well believe that his goal now is to be remembered in Panamanian history as one of the country's patriots, not one of the world's most notorious villains.

PAPAL NUNCIO JUAN LABOA, *Pope John Paul II's ambassador to Panama, speaking with guests at his residence.*

After thirty months of General Noriega's becoming more and more of an irritant in the eyes of the United States, Operation Just Cause finally succeeded in removing him from power.

FILES AND FILE DRAWERS
in one of General Noriega's
offices were incinerated
in the invasion.

SITTING ROOM
adjoining General
Noriega's office
at Paitilla Airport.

PANAMA'S MILITARY MUSEUM
(the Casa del Recuerdo) stands in ruins.
It was formerly one of General Omar Torrijos's
homes and was often used by
General Noriega for meetings.

NICARAGUAN EMBASSY
*under U.S. watch. Another
Nicaraguan diplomatic facility
was later searched in what
President Bush called a screw-up.*

PERUVIAN EMBASSY *was surrounded
by U.S. troops. Marcela Tazón,General
Noriega's secretary, eventually took
refuge there.*

U.S. RANGER, *armed with M-16 rifle and attached grenade launcher, maintains watch outside of Papal Mission.*

DELTA FORCE COMMANDO
*focuses his binoculars on the Papal
Nuncio's residence below.*

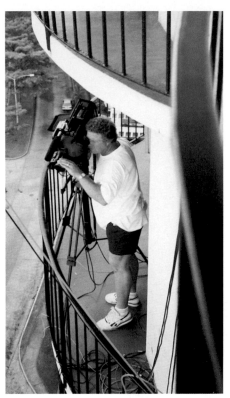

ABC-TV CAMERAMAN *hoping to catch some action at the Nunciatura from his Holiday Inn balcony.*

THE NUNCIATURA *is isolated by U.S. military forces once General Noriega's presence inside became known. So many PDF officers had preceded Noriega there that the Papal Nuncio had to engage a catering firm to feed some 40 unexpected guests.*

CNN STILL PHOTOGRAPHER *maintaining same vigil from different balcony.*

TROOPS POSITIONED *at and around the Nunicatura.*

The Papal mission is located in the well-to-do residential area of Panama City called Punta Paitilla.

MILITARY POLICEMAN
takes up his watch under the watchful eyes of some ladies.

FATHER SHOWS SON
features of an Armored Personnel Carrier.

CHEWING ON THIS PARTICULAR COLONEL
*was happy duty for these GIs. The food was
purchased for the soldiers by Panamanians
living in the Punta Paitilla area.*

GIRL WATCHING *helped fill the hours of waiting for
something to happen inside the Nunciatura.*

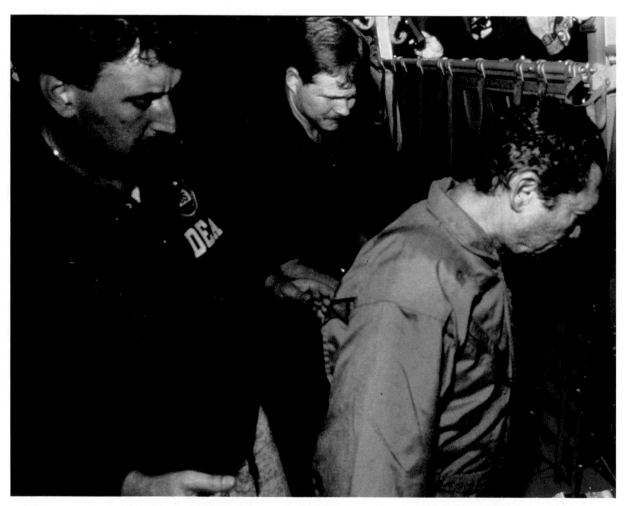

GENERAL MANUEL A. NORIEGA *in U.S. custody.*

PINEAPPLE serves as head of this effigy, while sign reads: "Noriega Your Time Has Come."

AMERICAN SOLDIER *chats with ladies in front of banner: "No Exile. Noriega Assassin. Justice for Panama."*

"THIS CRAP IS OVER"—*Panamanian Vice President Guillermo Ford's pointed declaration—is painted on side of U.S. military vehicle.*

SIGN TUCKED INTO BARBED WIRE *near Papal Nuncio's residence.*

LAWRENCE EAGLEBURGER, *Deputy Secretary of State, in Panama in part to help get Noriega out of the Nunciatura, shows no evident concern for the "No Smoking" sign behind him.*

A PANAMANIAN BOY PLAYS WAR
*against a target shaped like a
U.S.soldier sometime before
the U.S. invasion.*

**WAR WAS NO GAME
TO THE 82ND AIRBORNE**
*as it returns home to Ft. Bragg after the
success of the Panamanian operation.*

CONCLUSION

While many wars have been fought to acquire or defend *foreign* territory, the invasion of Panama may be one of the first wars ever fought to secure *domestic* approval.

PRESIDENT BUSH AND GENERAL POWELL *conferring on U.S. options prior to the invasion of Panama.*

It is hard to draw any other conclusion from the events of December 20, 1989, to January 3, 1990. Look at the four reasons given for undertaking the action:

- *The protection of American lives.* Hardly a credible excuse for the invasion since relatively few of the 40,000 American citizens living off of the U.S. military bases reported feeling in any imminent kind of danger.

117

- *The enforcement of the Panama Canal Treaties.* Unnecessary in light of the fact that the Canal had not been threatened by anyone and least of all by Panamanians.

- *The restoration of democracy.* Difficult to do when Panama has never had much of a tradition of democracy and the people were clamoring for nothing more than to be rid of General Noriega and to be able to get back to a reasonable level of economic activity.

- *Bringing General Noriega to justice.* Not something the United States wanted to do as much as it wanted to remove him from power.

If the four objectives as stated for the invasion were not really worth achieving, why then did the American people as well as Panamanians so overwhelmingly approve it?

In a word, because it *worked*—quickly, convincingly, and overwhelmingly to demonstrate that the United States could still draw a line in the sand that others would think about before crossing.

APPRECIATION FOR SUCCESS *is registered in the smile of this Panamanian lady.*

Any complaints that it may have been unnecessary, excessive, or ultimately damaging to more important U.S. international interests were quickly dismissed as carping or ignored as irrelevant. That may be true. But at some point Americans will need to look closely at aspects of the Panama invasion:

- *Take the matter of American overseas bases.* Will other countries now be reluctant to have them on their soil for fear that they will be used, like the U.S. bases in Panama were used, to intervene in the very society that had given permission for them to be there in the first place?

- *Take the matter of illegal drugs.* Will other countries now refuse to cooperate with the United States to avoid providing facilities for U.S. forces that might also be used against their own governments or to politically embarrass them?

- *Take the matter of foreign aid:* Will the amount pledged to Panama—to help repair damage done by the invasion and to right an economy devastated by sanctions—drain too much money away from other U.S. assistance programs needed in Eastern Europe and on-going in the Middle East, Central America, and the Far East or will the United States eventually have to adjust its promise to Panama to a much lower figure?

- *Take the question of the extraterritoriality of U.S. laws:* Will other countries continue to cooperate with American law enforcement officials if the United States continues to insist on the right to enforce its laws outside of the United States with its own police forces or through armed intervention?

There is another fundamental question that arises from the invasion. Americans have tended to treat Panama as a virtual *territory* of the United States because of the Panama Canal. Panamanians, on the other hand, have been proud of the *sovereign* role their country has long played in international commerce and communication. Will the fundamental disparity in these viewpoints fuel clashes between the two nations in the future as it has in the past?

While nearly all Panamanians deeply appreciate being released from the extraordinary economic pressures that General Noriega's presence eventually imposed on them, Americans should not expect their relationship with Panama to be forever dictated by a feeling of gratitude for the sacrifices and successes of America's military action.

But all of this relates to matters of America's international standing. In terms of *domestic* politics, the success of the invasion was overwhelming. That is both interesting and dangerous. Just as negative campaigning achieved great acceptance among professionals because practitioners tended to win their election campaigns, so successfully attacking smaller countries—as Ronald Reagan did in Grenada and Margaret Thatcher did in the Falklands, but Jimmy Carter failed to do in Iran—may be seen by future leaders as the required thing to do to secure reelection.

There was one other factor at work in the Panama situation. During most of 1989, the American people were frustrated that their government couldn't do more in Eastern Europe and didn't do more in China. Panama gave their government a chance to act like a great power and the Bush Administration took that chance. Because of the splendid way the U.S. military forces executed the mission they were given, the United States came away from the operation looking and feeling like a great power.

It is. It has been since World War II. The fact that ninety per cent of Americans approved of what their government did in Panama seemed an indication to many in Washington that what they did was *right*. Unfortunately, it is an MBA mentality invading politics. Politicians now tend to hold a finger in the air to determine what the "market" wants, then proceed to provide it at the lowest possible cost for the highest amount of benefits. Few today seem to be questioning whether what was *popular* in Panama was also *correct* for the United States.

History has often been critical of intervention. We will have to await the future to see how the American invasion of Panama is treaty in retrospect.

119

HELICOPTER HOVERS *over Panama Bay with the Pacific entrance to the Canal just beyond.*

EPILOGUE:
How a Dictator Was Taken Down

H-Hour for the invasion of Panama was scheduled for 1 a.m. on December 20, 1989. But Lt. Gen. Carl W. Stiner, the operational commander (*see photo, p. 43*), moved the start up fifteen minutes when Panamanian radio channels "came alive" with warnings for Panamanian Defense Forces to "get their guns and prepare to fight." There was nothing General Stiner could do, however, to move up the "drop time" of four thousand Army paratroopers, Rangers, and Green Berets who were on their way to Panama from four U. S. bases. These troops had to jump into heavy ground fire at Tocumen and Rio Hato, two military airfields where elite PDF units were stationed.

It was clear to Stiner that the mission had been "compromised," but he could only speculate on three possibilities for the leak: an overheard call from a State Department official to a friend at the Panama Canal Commission; a radio broadcast from Cuba; or U.S. news reports on unusual troop movements. "The security breach added to U.S. combat deaths and injuries," lamented Stiner.

Anatomy of an Assault

December 17: At 8:00 p.m. the Joint Chiefs of Staff order General Stiner to alert specified units for possible deployment. Within hours, Air Force cargo planes begin landing at Pope Air Force Base, adjacent to Fort Bragg, NC. Twenty-seven active and reserve flight crews from the Military Airlift Command come from air bases in fourteen states to haul the troops to Panama.

December 18: More than twenty-six hundred 82nd Airborne troopers and thirteen hundred Army Rangers are moved to the "Green Ramp" at Pope where they are isolated to prevent security leaks.

December 19: General Stiner flies to Panama to brief field commanders and make last minute changes in the plans for the top-secret operation. At 9:00 p.m. after an ice storm causes a three-hour delay in the transports leaving Pope Air Force Base, the first of twenty C-141 planeloads of paratroopers lifts off.

A plan to invade Panama had been readied for possible use during the Reagan Administration under the code name *Black Knight.* It was heavily reworked by Gen. Maxwell R. Thurman (*see photo, p. 42*), Commander-in-Chief of the U.S. Southern Command, after a coup attempt against Panama's Gen. Manuel A. Noriega had failed in October 1989. Thurman's review indicated that *Black Knight* would take too long to get up to speed. Thurman wanted any invasion to deliver a "knockout punch" in the first round and avoid subsequent bloody battles in the streets of Panama City.

Task Force Bayonet Gets Early Start

Col. Mike Snell—commander of the 193rd Infantry Brigade, which along with the mechanized 4th Battalion, 6th Infantry, formed the backbone of Task Force Bayonet—planned to isolate the headquarters of the Panamanian Defense Forces and then reduce the 400-man garrison with light infantry. But before his Task Force could cross its line of departure, heavy fire started coming from the Comandancia. (*See photo, p. 12*)

As the only "heavy" force with armored personnel carriers, Companies B and D of the 4th Battalion drew the assignment of leading the nighttime assault. The lead platoon of Company B lost eighteen men while advancing on the Comandancia. Two of the nation's highest decorations for conspicuous gallantry were awarded to soldiers from the 4th Battalion.

Spec. Roderick B. Ringstaff, a medic in D Company, was awarded the Silver Star for administering first aid to the wounded in his platoon, although he himself had received serious wounds to his arm and leg. Nearing exhaustion from loss of blood and still under devastating fire, Specialist Ringstaff dragged a wounded soldier to a medical evacuation vehicle. Although he physically collapsed at that point, Ringstaff continued to provide words of encouragement and moral support to members of his company.

The other Silver Star was awarded posthumously to Cpl. Ivan Perez who was listed as the first American soldier to be killed in action. As commander of the second armored personnel carrier in the lead platoon of Bravo company, Perez provided accurate and deadly suppressive fire from his .50 calibre machine gun, despite a hail of enemy fire aimed at his vehicle. When B Company's advance was halted by a roadblock, Corporal Perez maneuvered his vehicle close so he could cover the lead squad as it reduced the obstacle. Observers saw enemy fire striking all around Perez as he stood behind his machine gun until he was mortally wounded. Specialist Charles E. Berry was awarded the Bronze Star, one of the 7 men honored for gallantry in the face of the enemy at the Comandancia, for replacing Perez and providing suppressive fire against the enemy.

In addition to 2 Silver Stars and 7 Bronze Stars, the Army also awarded 14 Commendation Medals, 208 Purple Hearts, 899 Combat Infantry Badges, and 66 Combat Medical Badges to soldiers who participated in the Panama operation. The Navy awarded 13 Purple Hearts. The Marine Corps awarded 4 Purple Hearts, including one to Lt. Robert Paz who was killed just prior to the invasion.

There were two other important task forces in addition to TASK FORCE BAYONET. TASK FORCE ATLANTIC—made up of units from the 82nd Airborne Division and 7th Infantry Division—seized control of the Pacora River Bridge. TASK FORCE SEMPER FIDELIS, consisting of four hundred thirty Marines from three different units, cut off Panama City from countryside-based reinforcements (a lesson learned from the Soviet invasion of Afghanistan) by seizing control of the Bridge of the Americas over the Panama Canal. In controlling that bridge, the Marines also secured Howard Air Force Base, the staging area for the entire invasion. *(See photo, p. 36 and map, p. 23.)*

Despite Losses, Casualties Were Fewer Than Anticipated

In terms of casualties, the battle at the Comandancia was the bloodiest, with four soldiers killed and more than sixty wounded. But casualties could have been higher had it not been for a "shift in training focus" at the Panama-based 193rd Infantry Brigade from jungle warfare to urban warfare. A few weeks prior to the invasion, the 193rd conducted a full month of "live fire" exercises in a simulated urban setting at Fort Sherman in the Canal Zone.

"It takes live fire at the squad, platoon, and company level to build the kind of proficiency and confidence it takes on a tough mission like this one," said General Stiner. "You're not going to get a man to maneuver in front of his squad at night without fear of being shot in the back, unless he's done it in training," Stiner added whose own paratroopers honed their urban warfare skills at "Combat Town," a settlement of cinder-block buildings at Fort Bragg, North Carolina. It resembled what airborne troops would encounter at Tucumen, the military side of Omar Torrijos International Airport.

Army Rangers and Green Berets (Special Forces) practiced on simulated targets throughout the southeastern United States. Dress rehearsals for the invasion were held up until the day before D-Day (December 20, 1989). A and B Companies, 2nd Battalion, 75th Ranger Regiment from Fort Lewis, Washington, had just finished their last practice mission and returned to base only a few hours before they were ordered to fly back to Fort Benning, Georgia.

PDF Tougher Than Expected

Although the invasion's intensive fighting lasted only five or six hours, U.S. troops met more resistance than expected. General Stiner says a speech Noriega made to the PDF—when he told them they would see the bodies of their American adversaries floating down the Panama Canal— had the same effect on his men as Adolph Hitler's speeches did on German soldiers during the early days of World War II. "Young soldiers, especially the PDF, are very impressionable," said the thirty-one-year Army veteran, "But when the fighting began, PDF officers left their men to die." As evidence, Stiner pointed to the fact that the assault force didn't capture a single field grade officer on D-Day.

When the back of the PDF was broken, the paramilitary Dignity Battalions engaged in hit and run attacks. "They all had automatic weapons," said Stiner, "but U.S. intelligence couldn't determine how many Dingbats there were." It was not until D-Day Plus Three that U.S. forces captured documents that indicated there were actually a total of eighteen Dignity Battalions.

As General Stiner's men struggled to silence pockets of resistance, field commanders were forced to abandon conventional warfare techniques and fight a low-intensity type of urban combat. Street fighting and rooting out snipers in high rise buildings require a lot of manpower because units not only have to sweep the streets in front of them, but also must prevent infiltration from the rear. As insurance, additional troops were flown to Panama on D-Day Plus One and Two to bring the total U.S. military presence to more than 27,000. That was four and one-half times the number of troops President Ronald Reagan had used to invade Grenada in October 1983. But unlike the Grenada operation, which was thrown together in a couple of days, the Panama operation had been "in the works for months."

RADIO STATION *in this building was destroyed by an Apache helicopter from far offshore.*

A Measured Response in Panama

"Our philosophy from the beginning was to minimize casualties and damage," insisted General Stiner. To make sure civilian casualties were kept to a minimum, Stiner imposed strict rules of engagement on his troops. In order to use air strikes in Panama City, it took Stiner's approval. In order to fire artillery, it took the approval of a Major General. That's also the reason Stiner "smuggled in" six Apache helicopters capable of firing Hellfire missiles through a window at five miles in darkness. Stiner wanted weapons with "surgical accuracy." *(See photo to left.)*

For added firepower, four Sheridan light tanks were flown into Panama a week before the invasion, and hidden. *(See photo, p. 108)* Their 152mm cannons could be used in place of artillery. Eight other Sheridans were air dropped from C-141 Starlifters on the night of the invasion. However, two of the 42,000-pound tanks were lost when they collided in mid-air, causing parachutes attached to one of the tanks to collapse.

The Sheridan that fell 200 feet to the ground had to be "blown in place" because of live ammunition scattered inside the turret. The other tank went back to Fort Bragg for repairs. Last used in Viet Nam, the Sheridans are light and highly maneuverable—ideally suited to urban warfare. At one point, when snipers slowed down the advance on the Comandancia, Colonel Snell ordered the Sheridans to "put a tank round down their throat."

You Can Run, but You Can't Hide from SPECTRE

Aircraft from the 1st Special Operations Wing flew more than four hundred missions in Panama, involving in excess of twelve hundred hours flying time, but only one gunship suffered any battle damage. Seven AC-130H gunships from Hurlburt Field, Florida, and two AC-130A reserve gunships from Duke Airfield, Florida, were in the air December 20, flying support for U.S. troops below.

"SPECTRE took the roof off the Comandancia and punched holes in the upper floors with its One oh Five [105 mm howitzer]," said Colonel Snell. Walking through the ruins a week later, Chairman of the Joint Chiefs of Staff, General Colin Powell, said, "My eyes tell me there was a helluva fight here." *(See additional photos, pp. 10-11 and p. 41.)*

SPECTRE AC-130H

Although they couldn't see the SPECTRE's overhead, the PDF had no difficulty hearing their firepower whistling through the air—more than 17,000 rounds a minute. Gun camera footage showed anti-aircraft fire searching the skies over Panama, but PDF tracers never came close to a SPECTRE.

Unlike its Viet Nam-era cousins, the H-model SPECTREs do not have to fire tracer or incendiary rounds to mark targets. All of the targeting is done by low-light-level television cameras, laser target designators, and a two-kilowatt searchlight visible only to troops with night vision goggles. (Night vision goggles, by the way, were used for the first time in combat during the Panama operation and were praised by those who used them.)

When an ice storm in North Carolina delayed the departure of the 82nd Airborne Division from Fort Bragg by three hours, it made American troops late in taking control of the Pacora River Bridge on the road to Panama City from Fort Cimmarron where a key PDF unit was stationed. When that unit—Battalion 2000—attempted to carry the war into the heart of the Panamanian capital, a SPECTRE gunship obliterated the first nine vehicles in their convoy. The rest of the column returned to Fort Cimmarron.

While in Panama, I was the only correspondent allowed to fly a seven-hour mission aboard a SPECTRE. It happened on December 31, 1989.   "What a way to spend New Year's Eve," I thought as we lumbered down a Howard Air Force Base runway in a "flying bomb."

If we had to abort because of fire on takeoff, lead gunner Roger Betterelli said we had less than sixty seconds to scramble off the aircraft and run as fast as our legs could carry us. "After one minute, the 20mm starts cooking off, and then the 40mm starts exploding, and that sets off the 105s, so get your butt about two thousand yards from this bird," Betterelli said.

You could hear the 4,910-horsepower Allison turboprop engines on the modified C-130 Hercules "groan" as we lifted off the runway and climbed over the Bay of Panama where the crew wet bored (registered) the guns before relieving another gunship over Panama City. The 105mm howitzer in the rear of the C-130 was the first weapon to be fired. The four-man crew that serviced the weapon worked like Richard Petty's pit crew at the Daytona 500.

Technical Sergeant Betterelli lifted a forty pound round out of a rack behind the gun and slammed it into the howitzer's breech as another sergeant punched a series of buttons on an electronic display panel and lowered the weapon to its proper firing angle. "BOOOOM," bellowed the 105 as the converted field piece recoiled. Looking out a porthole near the rear ramp, I could see the white phosphorous round impact on a target range a mile below.

Once the 105 was registered, the crew moved forward to the twin 20mm Vulcan cannons. "Brrrr," chattered the 20mms, spewing empty shell casings into a wooden trough behind the firing curtain. *(See photo, p. 10.)* The Vulcan cannons sounded like jackhammers hitting concrete as the spent brass clears the spinning barrels. With a 5-second burst, SPECTRE can saturate a football field with 20mm slugs. As soon as the 40mm Bofors cannon amidships was wet bored, Lieutenant Col. Mike Guidry leveled off at fifty-five hundred feet over Panama City. "The 40mm is our most accurate weapon," explained Col. Guidry, "but the 105 is our weapon of choice."

The Air Force decided to experiment with a howitzer in its gunships when it became apparent that the North Vietnamese were able to repair trucks riddled with miniguns. "With the 105, there aren't enough pieces to put a truck back together again," laughed Guidry. During the next seven hours, we made at least 150 orbits over the Vatican Embassy where General Noriega was then located. The low-light-level television camera was so sensitive that we could see a man walking in total darkness a mile below us.

Really Big Air Show

The Panama operation was the most massive military undertaking since Viet Nam. The troops were airlifted to Panama by Military Airlift Command transports. The MAC aircraft came from twenty - one bases. Twenty-six separate squadrons, active and reserve, from the Strategic Air Command refueled the aircraft in route. A total of eleven missions were flown by C-130s, C-141s and C-5s on D-Day.

F-117A STEALTH FIGHTER

Eighty-four of the missions were air drops. Even though there was some question about the necessity of using the F-117A, a stealth fighter, General Stiner accepted Air Force assurances that the plane would "stun, disorient and confuse" the PDF without killing them. "We had to take down a government one day, and the next day tell the people of Panama we're their friends," Stiner said. Six of the aircraft flew from Nellis Air Force Base in Nevada, requiring several mid-air refuelings each. Two dropped bombs, four never saw action. It was later reported by the Air Force that rather than pin-point accuracy—as General Stiner had been promised—one of the planes actually missed its target by a considerable distance.

Airborne Action

The 1st Ranger Battalion from Hunter Army Airfield, Georgia, and a company from the 3rd Ranger Battalion at Fort Benning, Georgia, secured Torrijos International Airport and the adjoining military field at Tocumen.

Staff Sgt. Johnnie Houston, jumpmaster in one of the C-141 Starlifters, said his men met heavy resistance on the ground at Tocumen, but had no difficulty seizing the airfield. The Rangers were followed to Torrijos International Airport forty-five minutes later by the 82nd Airborne Division. Spec. 4 Melvin Handy from Gafney, South Carolina, had the distinction of being the first member of his unit to jump into combat. The twenty-three-year-old father of three children admitted he was scared as he jumped in the inky darkness at five hundred feet. "There was barely enough time for the parachute to deploy before hitting the ground," said Handy.

Combat jumps like the one at Tocumen are always costly in terms of manpower. That's why units jump at 106 per cent of their manning level. More than two hundred injuries were sustained on the drops. Most of the injuries were broken bones and badly sprained or twisted knees and ankles. The injury rate in Panama among paratroopers was six times what it is under training conditions. For one thing, training jumps are made at eight hundred feet. To minimize exposure to ground fire, airborne units jumped from only five hundred feet in Panama. Some soldiers apparently "freaked out" at the sight of so much ground fire and forgot to release their one hundred pound rucksacks attached on 20-foot tethers. As a result, some men fell like "lead sinkers" onto concrete runways creating an orthopedist's nightmare.

There was more than proper paratroop techniques to worry about at Rio Hato, a PDF base ninety miles southwest of Panama City. "When we jumped in, they [SPECTREs] had knocked out the anti-aircraft guns," said Pfc. Dean Hohl from Freeport, Illinois, "but even without the anti-aircraft fire, all of the transports that took us in, sustained battle damage."

"Some of the guys in my plane were hit while hooked up to jump," said Pfc. Chris Campbell from The Woodlands, Texas. One Ranger was shot in the back of the head as he stood in line to jump. Buddies had to step over him as they went out the door, but the soldier survived. Four other Rangers were killed in action at Rio Hato. One, Pfc. John Price from Ft. Lewis, Washington, would have celebrated his twenty-third birthday on Christmas Eve had he not been killed.

Even after the Rangers secured Rio Hato, PDF personnel who survived the initial assault tested the perimeter, but their probing was beaten back by SPECTRE whose target acquisition cameras turned the night to day. "We could see fountains of sparks flying as SPECTRE hosed down the airfield," said Hohl. Two hours after the parachute drop, U.S. Air Force transports were landing at Rio Hato bringing in additional equipment for the Rangers.

Instant Cash

A U.S. Army bounty program resulted in some seven thousand assault rifles, pistols, shotguns, hand grenades, rocket launchers, and an assortment of ammunition being exchanged for cash. Prices ranged from $25 for a hand grenade to $75 for a pistol to $150 for an automatic rifle. One man was paid $5,000 for an armored car he turned in—one of thirty-three armored vehicles captured or confiscated during Operation Just Cause.

Panamanians lined up by the hundreds outside a recreation center in Panama City where AK-47s, M-16s, APGs and other weapons were sold to the American forces with no questions asked. Most of the weapons I saw lying on the floor of the recreation center were covered with mud, indicating that they may have been discarded by the PDF. *(See photo montage, p. 45.)*

Overall, U.S. forces took in more than 52,000 weapons, many stockpiled in large caches throughout the country or in apartments and private homes. They found:

- 125 machine guns stashed in a sewer,
- 6,000 weapons in a huge cache at Rio Hato, and
- 16,000 weapons three hundred miles from Panama City.

More than 10,000 of the weapons were AK-47s, some still covered with cosmoline and concealed in crates marked "surveying tools." U.S. forces also seized more than 600 tons of ammunition and 80,000 pounds of explosives in a bunker along the Atlantic coast near Colon.

The size of the cache surprised Army officials; there were enough weapons to give every Panamanian soldier at least ten.

Lessons Learned in Panama

Senator Sam Nunn (D-GA) who chairs the Senate Armed Services Committee learned that a lot of the most useful U.S. equipment used in Panama was not new. "The reason the older equipment was better," said Nunn, "was because it was lighter." And that should tell Congress something about military procurement in the future. "We're going to have to have more mobility, and we're going to have to have lighter forces that can be transported quickly to places like Panama." said Nunn.

Although General Stiner says he didn't learn a thing, "tactically speaking," during the Panama operation, the Army realized it must increase urban warfare training. The Army also needs to increase the number of troops who specialize in "civil affairs," such as government administration. More than two thousand Army Reserve Civil Affairs personnel, or about forty per cent of the Civil Affairs resources, were committed to restoring Panama's social and legal infrastructure. When you "take down" a dictator like Noriega, you take down all forms of government with him, including law enforcement. After the invasion, the only police on the streets of Panama were a few U.S. MPs. *(See photos, pp. 76-79, 110, and 129.)*

MARINE LIGHT ARMORED VEHICE *in action in Panama.*

Although the military operation in Panama was mainly an "Army show," Marines played a key role in Operation Just Cause and learned some lessons in the process. An armored infantry task force comprised of a Light Armored Infantry (LAI) unit and a Fleet Anti-terrorist Security Team (FAST) launched a reconnaissance in force on D-Day. The target was La Chorrera, a town where a force loyal to General Noriega was located. When the dust settled from a roadblock destroyed by air support, the PDF was nowhere in sight. They had left town. *(See map, p. 19)*

Ever since the Marine Corps formed an LAI Battalion in 1984, planners had wondered how effective its 14-ton amphibious vehicles would be in combat. Now Washington no longer has to wonder. The Light Armored Vehicles (LAVs) received high marks in Panama. Unlike slower Armored Personnel Carriers, fast moving, rubber-tired LAVs were ideally suited to urban warfare. Although its armor is only an inch and a half thick, the LAV more than makes up for its lack of protection with speed, firepower, and mobility.

The Media

While the Pentagon War Pool arrived in Panama four hours after the fighting began—and were kept closeted in a windowless room at Fort Clayton in "fear" for their safety—a handful of correspondents, including my *NBC* radio colleague, Laura Brooks, was already there. *(See photo of Laura Brooks, p. 29.)*

Brooks, Lindsey Gruson of The *New York Times* and Paul Iredal of the *Reuters* News Agency, were watching the invasion from the cabana area at the Marriott Hotel when they saw "a man wearing a black ski mask and camouflage pants and carrying an automatic assault rifle run across the patio."

The reporters crouched, but the gunman spotted them. Gruson's account of their capture was chilling. "Out! Out!" the gunman shrieked aiming his AK-47 assault rifle. "We're coming!" the reporters shouted through the open patio window. "We don't have any weapons."

Brooks and her colleagues were ordered to lie face down by the gunman who demanded to know their nationality. After going through Brooks's handbag, the gunman handed it back to her. "You see, I'm not interested in your money," he said, "We've been ordered to take hostages." But the gunman eventually left on his own.

When members of TASK FORCE PACIFIC moved in the day after the invasion to rescue 14 other Americans who had barricaded themselves in the basement of the hotel, shooting broke out. A Spanish photographer was killed, and a photographer on assignment for *Newsweek* Magazine was seriously wounded in the action.

Good Morning, Panama

"We ran him hard," said General Stiner of the four-day search for General Noriega, "but he remained one step ahead of us." When Noriega slipped into the Vatican Embassy on Christmas Eve, the diplomatic compound became his box canyon. While Noriega remained in a windowless six by ten-foot room at the rear of the embassy, U.S. troops bombarded the area with rock and roll music. Contrary to press reports, however, the ear-shattering music was not aimed at Noriega. Instead, the loudspeakers were aim at rooms 600 and 601 at the Holiday Inn, which overlooks the embassy. *(See photos, pp. 100 and 106-107.)*

My colleague Bob Witten and I had been using these rooms to monitor "comings and goings" at the embassy below our balconies. It wasn't until two plainclothes special agents from the Department of Defense (DOD) armed with automatic weapons entered our rooms and said, "Freeze," that we realized *we* were the target of the psychological warfare.

The agents informed us that we had been under surveillance for three days. "You guys have been acting very strange," said one of the agents who held a cocked 9mm Baretta, "and we suspect you are conducting hostile intelligence."

We assured the DOD agents that the "shotgun" microphone we had sitting on the balcony was incapable of "eavesdropping" on conversations being held two hundred yards away at the gate to the Vatican Embassy. After examining our passports and searching our rooms, the agents left, apparently satisfied we were not spying on soldiers in the street below. But the music continued to rattle the sliding glass doors of our rooms. "Good Morning, Panama," said a would-be disc jockey as he cranked up the volume and played songs such as *No Place To Run*, *Voodoo Child*, *You're No Good*, and *Jailhouse Rock*. Bob and I didn't sleep for forty-eight hours, and neither did the Papal Nuncio who finally called the U.S. Ambassador and told him to please "stop the noise."

If the music was designed to rattle Noriega, it apparently failed, because the Papal Nuncio said Noriega slept like a baby. Noriega stayed in his room at the embassy for ten days. During that time the deposed dictator showed no signs of leaving. On the afternoon of January 3, however, a huge rally was held on Avenida Balboa within earshot of the Vatican Embassy. *(See photos, pp. 94-96).* Pressure was building to resolve the situation.

At 8:50 p.m. as I returned to my room in the Holiday Inn to advise my desk in Washington that "things were moving very fast," Noriega, accompanied by the Papal Nuncio, walked to the front gate of the embassy and surrendered to Maj. Gen. Marc Cisneros, deputy head of the U.S. Southern Command. Noriega was then taken to a nearby school soccer field where he was put aboard a Black Hawk helicopter and flown to Howard Air Force Base. There he was arrested by officials of the Drug Enforcement Administration and flown to the United States. *(See photo, p. 112.)*

Within fifteen minutes of Noriega's surrender, Panamanians were on the balconies of high rise condominiums in Paitilla and on the streets below banging pots and pans and celebrating. It was like the Fourth of July and New Year's Eve all wrapped into one evening. U.S. troops celebrated with citizens in the streets—waving tiny American and Panamanian flags. *(See photos, pp. 88-93.)*

Before Noriega was led off the C-130 Hercules at Homestead Air Force Base near Miami, he autographed the navigator's chart. The inscription read, "Buen Viaje" (the Spanish equivalent of Bon Voyage) and was signed: "M. Noriega, 4 Jan 1990."

Differences With Other Conflicts

For President Bush, the invasion of Panama, or "liberation" as some Panamanians called it, constituted a Presidential "Rite of Passage." For better or worse, U.S. Presidents have felt the need to show the world early on in their terms that they can use a big stick when necessary. John F. Kennedy did it during the Cuban Missile crisis; Lyndon Johnson and Richard Nixon did it during the Viet Nam War; Gerald Ford did it during the Mayaguez affair; Ronald Reagan did it in Grenada; and now Mr. Bush has done it in Panama.

Unlike the war in Viet Nam, armed intervention in Panama was popular with the folks at home. It also had a clearly defined set of military objectives and there's no question in the minds of any of the men and women who were in Panama who won this war.

Yes, 771 women were involved in the Panama operation. And for the first time women, who comprise eleven per cent of the U.S. armed forces, engaged hostile troops. A platoon of MPs from the 988th Military Police Company under the command of Capt. Linda L. Bray became involved in a firefight with Panamanian soldiers at a dog kennel near Panama City. The exploits of Bray's platoon rekindled debate in Congress over whether women should be involved in combat. A senior officer at the Pentagon said there was no intention of using women in combat. "They just happened to be in a combat zone," he said, "and Captain Bray probably wishes the whole thing hadn't happened. After all, who wants to be remembered for capturing a dog kennel."

FEMALE MP *on duty in Panama.*

High Marks for the Military

"From a professional military point of view, this operation will go down as a brilliant success," declared retired Army Chief of Staff Gen. Edward Meyer. He added: "It was probably the best conceived military operation since World War Two." It was certainly better conceived than the invasion of Grenada in 1983. That operation was thrown together in a few days. One example of the problems encountered: Navy commanders could not talk to their counterparts in the Army and Air Force, because their radios were incompatible. On a scale of 1-to-10, General Thomas Kelly—one of the Pentagon planners—gave the Panama operation an unconditional "10."

"I think it was the most professionally executed operation that I have seen in 33 years of military service," said Kelly. While he said that the battle plan was "bold and beautifully executed," the operation was certainly not flawless. Paratroopers missed their landing zone at Tocumen, winding up in swamp grass over their heads along with "enough equipment for a brigade" stuck in the muck. Commanders blamed poor aerial reconnaissance.

In another instance, it took more than three hours to secure the U.S. Embassy in Panama City after it came under a rocket attack by the PDF. *(See photo, p. 28)*. Four of the explosive warheads penetrated the building, wreaking havoc among the eight-man Marine guard who were lightly armed.

One of the thirty civilians in the building at the time of the attack told me: "The Army left us there to die, and had no intention of coming to our aid until we got on the telephone to the Pentagon, and demanded protection." "We could have been captured or killed," said the civilian who wished to remain anonymous, "if the PDF had followed up on the RPG attack." Even after an armored column arrived at the embassy, the commander wanted to move on after finding no evidence of the PDF. But another "frantic call" to Washington kept the cordon of steel around the diplomatic compound. In fact, the armor remained for the next two weeks until all danger had subsided.

Another oversight prevents the Panama operation from receiving a perfect "10." U.S. forces failed to secure a government radio station during the invasion and were surprised to hear General Noriega on the air saluting Panamanians who were resisting. "We must resist and advance," said Noriega. "Our slogan is to win or die, not one step back." It wasn't until almost twenty-four hours later that U.S. forces attacked the building where Panamanian national radio had been broadcasting appeals to resist efforts to capture General Noriega.

Furthermore, U.S. forces failed to protect the business district of Panama city and the docks at Colon from looters who carried off millions of dollars worth of merchandise. *(See photos, pp. 55-72.)* One electronics store lost $7.5 million in merchandise, including credit card receipts from the previous day's sales. And finally, the Panama operation does not deserve an unconditional 10 because it failed to achieve its major objective—the *capture* of Manuel Noriega. The United States was "powerless" to enter the Vatican Embassy and pull him out by the scruff of the neck. U.S. forces had to wait until the dejected dictator decided it was time to surrender.

So, unlike Kelly's scorecard, mine gives the Panama operation a "9," not a "10." But that's a high mark in any endeavor and something the whole country can take pride in.

Ross W. Simpson

APPENDIX

TWENTY-THREE U.S. SERVICEMEN DIED IN COMBAT DURING THE INVASION OF PANAMA.

PRIVATE JAMES TABOR, 18, Montrose, CO. Headquarters and Headquarters Co., 4th Bn., 325th Parachute Infantry Regt., 82nd Airborne Div., Fort Bragg, NC.

PRIVATE FIRST CLASS MARTIN DENSON, 21, Abilene,TX. B Co., 1st Bn,. 504th Parachute Infantry Regt., 82nd Airborne Div., Fort Bragg, NC.

SPECIALIST JERRY DAVES, 20, North Carolina. Headquarters and Headquarters Co., 1st Bn., 504th Parachute Infantry Regt., 82nd Airborne Div., Fort Bragg, NC.

SPECIALIST ALEJANDRO MANRIQUELOZANO, 30, Lauderhill, FL. D Co., 2nd Bn., 504th Parachute Infantry Regt., 82nd Airborne Div., Fort Bragg, NC.

STAFF SERGEANT LARRY BARNARD, 29, Hallstead, PA. B Co., 3rd Bn., 75th Ranger Regt., Fort Benning, GA.

PRIVATE FIRST CLASS ROY BROWN, JR., 19, Buena Park, CA. A Co., 3rd Bn., 75th Ranger Regt., Fort Benning, GA.

SPECIALIST PHILLIP LEAR, 21, Westminister, SC. B Co., 2nd Bn., 75th Ranger Regt., Fort Lewis, WA.

PRIVATE FIRST CLASS JAMES MARKWELL, 21, Cincinnati, OH. Headquarters and Headquarters Co., 1st Bn., 75th Ranger Regt., Hunter Army Airfield, GA.

PRIVATE FIRST CLASS JOHN M. PRICE, 23, Conover, WI. A Co., 2nd Bn., 75th Ranger Regt., Fort Lewis, WA.

FIRST LIEUTENANT JOHN HUNTER, 30, Victor, MT. Headquarters and Support Co., 160th Special Operations Aviation Group (Airborne), Fort Campbell, KY.

CHIEF WARRANT OFFICER WILSON B. OWENS, 29, Myrtle Beach, SC. 160th Special Operations Aviation Group (Airborne), Fort Campbell, KY.

CHIEF WARRANT OFFICER ANDREW PORTER, 25, Saint Clair, MI. B Co., 1st Bn., 123rd Aviation Regt., 7th Infantry Div., Fort Ord, CA.

LIEUTENANT (JUNIOR GRADE) JOHN P. CONNORS, 25, Arlington, MA. Navy SEAL, Little Creek, VA.

CHIEF ENGINEMAN DONALD L. MCFAUL, 32, San Diego, CA. Navy SEAL, Little Creek, VA.

BOATSWAIN'S MATE FIRST CLASS CHRISTOPHER TILGHMAN, 30, Kailua, HA. Navy SEAL, Little Creek, VA.

TORPEDOMAN'S MATE SECOND CLASS ISSAC G. RODRIGUEZ III, 24, Missouri City, TX. Navy SEAL, Little Creek, VA.

CORPORAL GARRETH C. ISAAK, 23, Greenville, SC. USMC, Camp Lejune, NC.

PRIVATE KENNETH SCOTT, 20, Princeton, WV. A Co., 4th Bn., 6th Infantry, 5th Infantry Div. (Mechanized), Fort Polk, LA.

CORPORAL IVAN PEREZ, 22, Pawtucket, RI, B Co., 4th Bn., 6th Infantry, 5th Infantry Div, (Mechanized), Fort Polk, LA.

SPECIALIST WILLIAM GIBBS, 22, Marina, CA. C Co., 4th Bn., 17th Infantry Regt., 7th Infantry Div., Fort Ord, CA.

SERGEANT MICHAEL DEBLOIS, 24, Dubach, LA. C Co., 1st Bn., 508th Infantry Regt., 193rd Infantry Bde., Panama.

PRIVATE FIRST CLASS VANCE COATS, 18, Great Falls, MT, Headquarters and Headquarters Co., 1st Bn., 508th Infantry Regt., 193rd Infantry Bde., Panama.

PRIVATE FIRST CLASS SCOTT ROTH, 19, Killeen, TX, 401st Military Police Co., Fort Hood, TX.

Another American name should be remembered. **MARINE FIRST LIEUTENANT ROBERT PAZ** *was shot and killed by members of the Panama Defense Forces on December 16, 1989. His death triggered the activities which led directly to the invasion.*

THREE AMERICAN CIVILIANS ALSO DIED IN THE FIGHTING

MRS. GERTRUDGE KANDI HELIN, a Department of Defense school teacher, was shot and killed as she and her husband, a Panama Canal Commission employee, were returning to their home.

RICHARD PAUL, the son of a Department of Defense school teacher, died of gunshot wounds received December 20 while returning home from a party.

RAYMOND DREGSETH, a Department of Defense computer science teacher, was first buried as "John Doe" on December 26. Dregseth was later exhumed and identified. He had been abducted from his home on December 20 by four gunmen claiming to be members of the Panama Defense Forces. Two of the gunmen said they were looking for Americans when they broke into Dregseth's apartment in the same Punta Paitilla building occupied by Manuel Noriega's mistress, Vicki Amado. Dregseth was the only American taken from the building. An unfortunate irony is that Victoria Dregseth, Raymond's wife, is the sister of Richard Paul's mother.

> **Many PANAMANIAN soldiers and civilians also died in the invasion. An accurate listing of these people has not yet been compiled—and may never be. We honor their memory and wish that their sacrifice might not have been.**

UNIT ROSTER FOR
OPERATION JUST CAUSE

MAJOR FORCES IN PANAMA PRIOR TO OPERATION JUST CAUSE

Army
5th Battalion, 87th Infantry Regiment, 193rd Infantry Brigade
1st Battalion, 508th Infantry (ABN), 193rd Infantry Brigade
4th Battalion, 6th Infantry, 5th Infantry Division (MECH), Ft.
     Polk, LA
2nd Battalion, 27th Infantry, 7th Infantry Division, Ft. Ord, CA
92nd Military Police Battalion
504th Military Police Battalion
3rd Battalion, 504th Infantry, 82nd Airborne Division, Ft. Bragg, NC

Marines
Marine Corps Security Force Co., Rodman, Panama
K Company, 3rd Battalion, 6th Marine Regiment, Camp Lejeune, NC
D Company, 2nd Light Armored Infantry Bn., Camp Lejeune, NC
Det., Brigade Service Spt. Group, Camp Lejune, N.C.
1st Fleet Anti-Terrorist Security Team (FAST) Plt., Norfolk, VA

Air Force
24th Communications Wing

MAJOR UNITS/ELEMENTS DEPLOYED TO PANAMA FOR OPERATION JUST CAUSE

Army
Composite brigade (units drawn from two brigades of the 82nd Airborne Division, Ft.
     Bragg,NC
1st Battalion, 75th Ranger Regiment, Ft. Stewart, GA
2nd Battalion, 75th Ranger Regiment, Ft. Lewis, WA
3rd Battalion, 75th Ranger Regiment, Ft. Benning, GA
2nd Brigade, 7th Infantry Division, Ft. Ord, CA
16th MP Brigade, Ft. Bragg, NC

Air Force
1st Special Operations Wing—Spectre Gunship
Hurlburt Field, FL; Duke Airfield, FL
4450th Tactical Group—117A Stealth Fighter
Nellis Air Force Base, NV

Strategic Air Command refueling (active & reserve)—26 separate squadrons from the following 14 bases:
Barksdale, LA; Eaker AFB, AK; Plattsburg AFB. NY; Robins AFB, GA; Grand Forks AFB, ND; Loring AFB, ME; Ellsworth AFB, SD; Altus AFB, OK; McConnell AFB, KN; Seymour-Johnson AFB, SC; March AFB, CA; Beale AFB, CA; Dyess AFB, TX; Grissom AFB, IN

Military Airlift Command transports (active & reserve)—27 units from the following 21 bases:
Travis AFB, CA; Norton AFB, CA; Channel Islands, CA; Westover AFB, MA; Andrews AFB, MD; Nashville, TN; McChord AFB, WA; Dover, DE; Wilmington, DE; Charleston AFB, SC; McGuire AFB, NJ; Little Rock, AK; Pope AFB, NC; Dyess AFB, TX; Kelly AFB, TX; NAS Dallas, TX; St. Joseph, MO; Charlotte, NC; Savannah, GA; Jackson, MS; Stewart AFB, NY

Military Airlift Command communications support—6 units deployed from the following bases:
Travis AFB, CA; Norton AFB, CA; Dover AFB, DE; Charleston AFB, SC; McGuire AFB, NJ; Dyess AFB,TX

Weather detachment deployed from Dover AFB, DE

Serial support units (cargo handlers)—7 from the following bases:
Dyess AFB, TX; Little Rock AFB, AK; Pope AFB, NC; Norton AFB, CA; Charleston AFB, SC; McGuire AFB, NJ

Navy
SEAL Unit, Little Creek, VA

ABOUT THE AUTHORS AND THIS BOOK

DAVID S. BEHAR and **GODFREY HARRIS** have been friends since 1967. They met when both were employed by Investors Overseas Services (IOS), an international financial company based in Geneva, Switzerland. Behar had come to manage the company's sales operations in Central America after merchandising various products along Panama's famed Central Avenue; Harris dealt with the company's governmental relations in Latin America, having been a university teacher, U.S. diplomat, and Presidential analyst prior to his association with IOS.

Soon after meeting in Panama, Harris and Behar discovered that they had much in common:

- Both had been born in England—Harris in London in 1937; Behar in Manchester in 1938.

- Both were moved by their parents from England to the safety of the Western Hemisphere at the outset of World War II—Harris to the United States; Behar to Panama.

- Both were part of a three-son family—Behar was the eldest in his family; Harris, the youngest.

To complete the parallels in their lives, both have watched three children grow and prosper (three boys for Harris; two boys and a girl for Behar).

GODFREY HARRIS WITH DAVID BEHAR *(l. to r.) in Panama.*

Since their days with IOS, Behar has built a career as an independent businessman with interests in real estate, finance, and wholesale services, while Harris has created an international public policy consulting firm headquartered in California. Along the way, they have been associated in a number of different innovative business ventures.

They began this project almost immediately after the invasion had ended. Behar had taken some six thousand photos during the U.S. operation and thought they should be preserved in some format. After Harris developed a detailed outline for a possible photo essay book, he joined Behar in Panama in March to review Behar's photographs and others he had acquired. Ross Simpson contributed some of the photos he had taken as well as those he was able to obtain from the Defense Department. After two cuts of the material, the photos were then reviewed with John Powers, the design and graphics consultant for the book. Two further cuts reduced the final selection to the 163 photographs that appear in this book.

The events unfolding in Panama between December 20, 1989, and January 3, 1990, were viewed by Behar and Harris in terms of their separate experiences and their vastly different observations of Panama. Over the next

ROSS W. SIMPSON doing a stand-up commentary in front of the Comandancia in Panama City.

several months, they fully expect that many new facts about the invasion will be revealed, dozens of fresh insights will emerge, and a host of equally valid interpretations of why things occurred as they did will gain currency. As a result, they believe that what they have presented here is not so much revealed truth as reasonable reflections.

ROSS W. SIMPSON looks at much of what he has presented in the Prologue and Epilogue in the same vein. Simpson met Behar soon after the invasion had begun—he had flown to Panama on December 26, 1990 from his base in Washington, DC, on assignment for Westwood One, the parent company of both the NBC Radio Network and the Mutual Broadcasting System. Simpson and Behar became instant friends as Behar guided Simpson around Panama and as they shared the danger and excitement of covering the invasion events together. Simpson is an award-winning radio correspondent, having served as a congressional correspondent, a floor reporter at Democratic and Republican National Conventions, and as the anchor of the evening news on Mutual radio. In addition to his field work in Panama, Simpson also covered the release of Nelson Mandela in South Africa, Hurricane Hugo in South Carolina, and the wild fires in Yellowstone National Park. He is perhaps most noted for his exclusive reporting after the assassination attempt on former President Ronald Reagan.

Despite the fact that both Behar and Harris—as well as Simpson—bring considerable expertise and background to this project, they had to have a lot of help to get an idea conceived in mid-January to completion by the end of May in the same year. Along the way they were assisted greatly by the following people:

- **RICHARD ARMSTRONG** reprocessed some of the color photographs.
- **NANCY BOSS ART** lent her always talented and sharp editorial eye and pencil to the project.
- **JOSEPH** and **VICTOR BEHAR** provided communication facilities and work space in Panama and carefully reviewed drafts of the book.
- **GINA BLANKENSHIP** guided the book's manufacturing process at Penguin Printing.
- **WILLIAM P. BUTLER** read the manuscript and made valuable suggestions at an early stage of the project.
- **LISA-ANNE CULP** provided important administrative and technical assistance.
- **DAVID** and **MICHAEL HARRIS** both kindly commented on the final draft of the book.
- **GREGREY HARRIS** provided ideas on layout choices and graphic concepts.
- **KENNITH HARRIS** created some of the maps used in the book and did much of the final typesetting.
- **SUSAN LAPHAM** gave us her experience and enthusiasm as our contact at Penguin Printing.
- **GREG J. MAYER** helped with the identification of military units and individual equipment.
- **COLONEL MIGUEL E. MONTEVERDE, SR.,** Director of Defense Information and his departmental staff—particularly Bob Bockman, Ken Carter, and Major Kathy Wood—researched facts and supplied photographs used in the book.
- **JAMIE PFEIFER** contributed to the cover design and worked on other aspects of the book.
- **JOHN POWERS,** a talented professional photographer as well as the book's graphic consultant, created the montage on p. 45 and shaped the panorama on pp. 94-95.
- **JAMES F. RAGAN, JR.** provided computer advice and valuable assistance.
- **CAPTAIN MITCHELL TOMS,** a member of the U.S. Southern Command's Public Information Office, was of help to both David S. Behar and Godfrey Harris in identifying some of the photographs.

- **ROSARIO TOWNSHEND DE GARCIA** translated most of the graffiti and signs, served as a copy editor, and did research for the book.
- **RITA M. ZENTNER DE FÁBREGA** provided secretarial assistance in Panama.

Because of the seven thousand miles, three time zones, and vastly different holiday schedules that separated Behar and Harris much of their work was conducted by phone or FAX at odd hours. As a result, both of their wives, Marcela Grobman de Behar and Barbara DeKovner-Mayer, deserve special recognition for their indulgence at the disruptions caused in *their* normal routines as well as for the special editorial help both gave to the project.

While David Behar took the vast number of photographs reproduced in the book—using a 35 mm Canon Sure Shot and Canon EOS camera with a variety of Kodak film—credit is also due to a number of others who contributed their photographic talent to ensure that we could offer a comprehensive view of the invasion. These people and the pages on which their work appears follows:

- **U.S. AIR FORCE TSGT H. H. DEFFNER,** *page 2.*
- **U. S. DEPARTMENT OF DEFENSE** (photographers unknown), *pages 13, 31, 37 (MAC), 112, 115, 117, 124, and 125.*
- **JOSÉ A. DOLLANDER L.,** *page 133.*
- **RAMON GATEÑO Z.,** *pages 14 (flare), 76 (bus), 120, and 140.*
- **JULIO CÉSAR GUERRA D. ,** *pages 12, 34 (burning building), 46, 102.*
- **JORGE MATSUFUJI ARAY,** *pages 68 (bicycle store) and 70 (Cuna family).*
- **PANAMA CANAL COMMISSION** (photographer unknown) *pages 18 and 21.*
- **ROSS W. SIMPSON**, *pages 10, 11, 16, 26, 32 (camouflage), 33 (detainee camp), 40, elements of the montage on 45, 50-51, 54, 100, and 129.*

The negatives for the pictures on pages 98, 99, and 115 (the boy playing war) were purchased outside of the looted offices of the Attorney General of Panama. These photos are believed to have been taken by Carlos Augusto Villalaz, the Attorney General of Panama, during the summer of 1989. One final note: the design at the end of each section— such as the one at the bottom of this page—is a reproduction of one of the fascinating and colorful designs (called *molas*) created by the Cuna Indians of the San Blas Islands of Panama.

While both Harris and Behar are deeply indebted for all the assistance they have received in completing this project, in the final analysis, of course, only they are responsible for its presentation. They realize that readers are just as likely to find a few memorable phrases and remarkable photographs as they are to discover some silly mistake or egregious error. Both Harris and Behar want everyone to know that while they are solely to blame for the latter, they are equally certain that they owe a debt of gratitude to someone for the former.

May 1990
Panama City, Panama
Los Angeles, California

BIBLIOGRAPHICAL NOTES

PROLOGUE and EPILOGUE

The background information developed by Ross W. Simpson for the Prologue and Epilogue sections was derived from his on-the-spot reporting in Panama between December 26, 1989 and January 16, 1990 and from research, after returning to the United States, among his sources on Capitol Hill, at the Pentagon, and with military specialists around the country. For additional details on SPECTRE, see his article, "Devil in Disguise," *Soldier of Fortune*, May 1990; for more on the Marine Corps role in the Panama operation, see his article, "Task Force Semper Fidelis," *Leatherneck*, March 1990.

INTRODUCTION

The concepts on Panamanian affairs presented in the Introduction emerge from experience, observations, research, and reporting by Godfrey Harris over the past 18 years. During that period, he has served as a consultant to the Foreign Policy Association of Panama and the Embassy of Panama in Washington, DC. Most of this work has been proprietary. Some, however, has been published. In particular, see Godfrey Harris, *Panama's Position: From the Threshold to the Present*, Asociación de Relaciones Internacionales, 1973, and Godfrey Harris, "The Panama Canal Problem," *Vital Issues*, January 1976.

For background on the Canal, see particularly David McCullogh, *Path Between the Seas: The Creation of the Panama Canal—1870-1914*, Simon & Shuster, 1977, and Uhrich Keller, *The Building of the Panama Canal in Historic Photographs*, Dover Publications, 1983.

For a comprehensive history of Panama in English refer to David Howarth, *Panama: 400 Years of Dreams and Cruelty*, McGraw Hill, 1966. For a useful review of U.S. dealings with Panama see Sheldon Liss, *The Canal: Aspects of United States-Panamanian Relations*, University of Notre Dame Press, 1967.

PROTECTING AMERICAN LIVES

Information on day-to-day events just prior to and during the invasion comes principally from following the reporting in the *Los Angeles Times*, the *New York Times*, the *Wall St. Journal* and the *Washington Post* and watching the coverage on the *CBS Evening News with Dan Rather* and *ABC's World News Tonight with Peter Jennings* from mid-December 1989 through the end of January 1990. Selective articles from this same period on the wires of Associated Press, United Press International, and the Reuters News Agency (through CompuServ) as well as broadcast feeds from CNN, C-SPAN and the CBS Radio Network were also available to Harris. Finally, he reviewed transcripts of the official statements released by the White House, the Defense Department, and the U.S. Southern Command.

Additional information used in the preparation of this book was developed by Godfrey Harris on a trip to Panama between March 1, 1990 and March 8, 1990. While there, he interviewed numerous Panamanians on their impressions and reactions to the events and aftermath of the invasion. For example, one detainee (held on suspicion that he knew about a weapons cache) called the conditions at the Empire Range facility "rudimentary"—sleeping on the ground, having to use slit trenches, and eating MREs (meals ready to eat).

For some comparisons between the PDF and the Israeli Defense Forces, as well as other background on the Israel connection, see Barbara DeKovner- Mayer, "Inside Panama and the Jewish Community," *The Jewish News*, September 1988.

For information on PDF wealth, see an article by Gabriel Lewis, the former Panamanian Ambassador to the United States, in the *Los Angeles Times*, July 31, 1987.

The question of the number of Panamanians who died in the invasion will probably never be resolved. The most authoritative investigation until now (and the basis for the numbers used in the book) was conducted by the Physicians for Human Rights, a New York-based, independent American group. Their report was issued on March 14, 1990.

Another unfolding story concerning the invasion deals with 8 Panamanian deaths involving American soldiers in non-combat circumstances. (See stories in the *Army Times* and the *Los Angeles Times* during the week of March 19, 1990.)

Finally, legal presentations connected to the drug related charges lodged against General Noriega are likely to reveal additional information about the invasion. In this regard, Frank Rubino, General Noriega's lead attorney, hinted on *This Week with David Brinkley* (January 7, 1990) that General Noriega may have sought designation as Panama's "Maximum Leader" for U.S. *legal* reasons rather than for Panamanian *political* purposes. Instead of simply matching a title once held by Omar Torrijos or gaining equality with other Latin American political leaders (as was first assumed), General Noriega may have wanted to become the equivalent of a "Chief of State" because U.S. law now treats those in such positions differently from foreign officials with lesser titles or duties.

The relationship of news to political events is painstakingly discussed in Herbert J. Gans, *Deciding What's News: A Study of CBS Evening News, NBC Nightly News, Newsweek and Time*, Pantheon Books, 1979. The importance of media perceptions to the play of events in Washington is well documented by Donald T. Regan, *For the Record: From Wall St. to Washington*, Harcourt Brace Javanovick 1988 and David A. Stockman, *The Triumph of Politics: Why the Reagan Revolution Failed*, Harper & Row, 1986.

Television critic Howard Rosenberg writes about the phenomenon of watching revolutions from hotel rooms—first noted in television coverage from Beijing in June 1989. He also points out that on-the-air reporting from the Marriott Hotel put special pressure "on U.S. forces to come to the rescue of a specific hotel." He suggests (correctly) that other Americans were in *other* hotels at the time of the invasion. Rosenberg concludes with a question: "Media first, others second?" (*Los Angeles Times*, December 21, 1989.)

ENFORCING THE PANAMA CANAL TREATIES

For good information on the Panamanian banking system, shipping registry, and the Colon Free Zone, we recommend, Kenneth J. Jones, *Panama Now*, Focus Publications (Int.) S.A., 1986 (and subsequent editions).

In addition, Godfrey Harris, *The Panamanian Perspective: A Bright Future Linked to a Rich Past*, Foreign Policy Association of Panama, 1987, looks at the role of the Canal in past and future Panamanian policy. For background on the 1977 treaty (known as the Torrijos/Carter Treaty in Panama and the Panama Canal Treaty in the United States), see Cyrus Vance, *Hard Choices: Critical Years in America's Foreign Policy*, Simon & Shuster, 1983, and Jimmy Carter, *Keeping Faith: Memoirs of a President*, Bantam Books, 1982.

For an understanding of the operation of the Canal itself, see the beautifully photographed and elegantly printed 75th Anniversary Commemorative Album, *Honoring the Past by Building the Future*, The Panama Canal Commission, 1989.

RESTORING THE DEMOCRACTIC PROCESS

For one of the most thoughtful articles on democracy and its role in the conduct of U.S. foreign policy, read Henry A. Kissinger, "Dealing from Reality," *Los Angeles Times*, November 22, 1987.

Information on the U.S. reaction to the the 1984 election of Nicolás Ardito Barletta comes from an interview with Mario Rognoni, the former Minister of Commerce and Industry of Panama and now one of its elected legislators, on March 4, 1990.

The President of Panama is known as Guillermo Endara *outside* of Panama, Guillermo Endara Galimany (his mother's surname) *inside* of Panama. We have used both versions, depending on whether the reference to Mr. Endara involves Panamanian matters or international matters.

The information on housing losses was chronicled in *Opinion Publica*, February 1990, a Panamanian periodical.

For background on the Civic Crusade, see Ricardo Arias Calderón, "Panama: Destination or Democracy," *Foreign Affairs*, Winter 1988.

One final note here: Rognoni told Harris that the feeling inside the Noriega camp was that the regime could not last in face of the abrogation of the May 1988 elections. Officials felt that pressure from within Panama, from other Latin American countries, and particularly from the United States would be too great for them to withstand. Rognoni said that in fact Noriega's people were surprised that their run continued for as many months as it did; their survival, in fact, may have emboldened them to believe that they could carry on even longer and that the December threats from the United States were just part of another elaborate bluff.

BRINGING GENERAL NORIEGA TO JUSTICE

Most of the impressions and data on U.S. dealings with General Noriega come from a manuscript by Godfrey Harris and Guillermo de St. Malo A., *The Panamanian Problem: How the Reagan and Bush Administrations Dealt with the Noriega Regime*. The book is expected to be published in 1991 by The Americas Group.

Noriega's support for Bush is documented in Lally Weymouth's article "Why is Elliott Abrams Picking on Panama's Noriega," *Washington Post*, October 11, 1987. Information about the 1988 agreement that fell through has been greatly embellished by Harris's discussions with ABC-TV's Peter Collins.

Some of the background on General Noriega comes from T. D. Allman's "Unnecessary Evil," *Vanity Fair*, May 1988.

Frederick Kempe's book, *Divorcing the Dictator: America's Bungled Affair With Noriega*, Putnam, 1990, differs in some respects from Rognoni's knowledge of events between December 19, 1989, and December 24, 1989. It could well be that the difference in perception stems from the fact that Kempe's sources appear to have been U.S. intelligence officials while Rognoni was dealing directly with the General in those days.

One story about the final arrangements for General Noriega to enter the Nunciatura is a case in point. Rognoni told Harris that for security reasons each step in his negotiations with Monsignor Laboa had to be relayed to the General through an intermediary. But Rognoni was having a problem. He told the Papal Nuncio: "You'll have to call me every half-hour. I can't get through. Your line is always busy." The Vatican's diplomat responded that with 37 PDF officers already in the residence, it was no wonder the phone was in use. But he would see to it that the line was cleared long enough for him to call Rognoni.

Despite the understandable differences with Rognoni on events during the last days, Kempe has additional data and stories on past Noriega connections to the United States of great interest. But so does Seymour M. Hersh in his article "The Creation of a Thug: Our Man in Panama," *Life Magazine*, March 1990. Hersh suggests that a coup attempt in 1970 against Omar Torrijos (an attempt that Manuel Antonio Noriega helped to thwart) was instigated by the CIA. According to Hersh, the CIA was jealous over the information being developed and control being exercised by Army intelligence in Panama. To regain its position as the lead American foreign intelligence source on the Isthmus, the agency wanted *its* man running the National Guard. The CIA failed.

MARIO ROGNONI *with a U.S. soldier behind him.*

For equally fascinating tidbits of information and linkages to all sorts of U.S. overseas operations, see Leslie Cockburn's *Out of Control: The Story of the Reagan Administration's Secret War in Nicaragua, the Illegal Arms Pipeline, and the Contra Connection*, Atlantic Monthly, 1987.

CONCLUSION

For a thoughtful and beautifully composed essay on the invasion, read Michael Kinsley, "Speak Softly and Carry a Cage," *Time Magazine*, January 22, 1990. It is Kinsley who first raises the point that in proportion to its size Panama lost more people in a few days than the United States lost in seven year in the Viet Nam War. (Kinsley also writes the TRB column in the *New Republic.)*

For another review of all the major issues involved in the invasion, see "Battle for Panama," a special supplement from *The Miami Herald*, March 11, 1990.

It should also must be noted that on March 6, 1990, President Endara told the NBC *Today* program that Panama's *economic* condition has become far worse since the invasion.

First Monday, the voice of the Republican Party, reviews Operation Just Cause with some glaring inaccuracies, but notes that the support of the American people for the Panama operation was a virtually unanimous ninety-two per cent. (Spring 1990.)

Finally, in terms of the future, Panamanians point out that while the majority of people in the cities of Panama and Colon had eventually come to oppose the Noriega regime, the people in the countryside—comprising forty per cent of Panama's population— probably continued to favor his government. These people—cut off from information, supplies, and contact at the time of the invasion—may be cut off in the future as resources are devoted to the rebuilding process in Panama's two principal cities.

AUTHORS

Many of the photographs that Behar managed to take were made possible by help he received from Staff Sgt. Johnnie Houston in the early days of the invasion.

Because we discuss the use of a mola design as a typographical device, some readers may want more information on this particular form of folk craft. We recommend a catalog published by the Textile Museum of Washington, DC called *Molas: Art of the Cuna Indians*, published in 1973. In addition, see also John Canaday, "Artistry via Needle From Panama Islands," The *New York Times*, December 30, 1968.

INDEX